Biblical Leadership

Based on the Life of Moses,

for Business and Everyday

Eric M. Towler, PhD, PMP

ISBN: 979-8-218-51896-7

DEDICATION

This work is dedicated to memory of my beloved teacher and friend, Rabbi Morris Kosman, z"l, who was the spiritual leader of Beth Sholom Congregation in Frederick, MD from 1961 until January 2010, when he became rabbi emeritus and moved to Baltimore. Rabbi Kosman embodied all the attributes of a leader and teacher. Like countless others, I was privileged and honored to have known him and benefitted from his loving, caring and nurturing spirit.

CONTENTS

ACKNOWLEDGEMENTS

The first acknowledgement, of course, goes to HaKadosh Baruch Hu for providing everything to make this work possible. I am deeply indebted to Rabbi Ely Allen of Hesder Yeshiva Lev HaTorah (Beit Shemesh, Israel) for the initial encouragement that this work could add value, for recommending several of the sources used for this book and for providing feedback on the content. Rabbi Dovid Rosenbaum of Young Israel Shomrei Emunah (Silver Spring, MD) was instrumental in not only providing encouragement but also recommending the Chumash Mesoras Harav as a valuable resource. My son, Eitan Ilan, not only recommended the Mesoras HaRav sources but also encouraged me to "stop reading and start writing already."   Both my wife, Shifra bat Avraham, and my mother, Tzivia Miriam bat Chanoch, spent a great deal of time editing the manuscript for syntax and clarity. Finally, the beautiful original illustrations, including the book cover ("The Eternal Nature of Leadership"), were the creation of my talented daughter, Shayna Rochel.

INTRODUCTION

Thesis statement

Leadership skills are required at all levels of daily engagement whether dealing with friends, teams, departments, or major corporations (Cope, 2012). Leadership itself is nearly universally recognized as the ability to ***influence*** others despite lack of formal authority (for example see (A. R. Cohen & Bradford, 1990; Sacks, 2016)). However, the ***attributes*** of a good leader do not enjoy such a consensus. Indeed, the past several decades have seen an explosion of books on leadership and attributes of a good leader (George, 2003; Goleman, 2006; Maxwell, 2007, and others). Given the abundance of works on leadership, one may wonder if there is any more to add, or if there is a more tried-and-true reference of what constitutes a leader, not to mention how to become a leader. That is what this work aims to explore.

Goal of this work

The goal of this work is to address leadership characteristics based on a 3000-year-old source, namely the five books of Moses (aka the "Torah"), and touch briefly on the topic of training oneself to become a leader. The rationale for this source is that it is the basis of three of the world's major religions (Judaism, Islam, and Christianity) and maybe even Hinduism as well (Seinfeld, 2010). The fact that there are books (Brown, 2008) and even a journal[1] dedicated to

---

[1] https://www.lookstein.org/about-the-jel-journal/

"Jewish Leadership" (based on Torah) further supports the use of this text as a reference.

The primary source for this work is the Torah itself with commentary by the 11th/12th century sage known as Rashi[2] (Herczeg, 1999). Secondary sources include a contemporary of Rashi, the Ramban[3] (Ben Nachman, 2010), a 19th/20th century sage known by his famous book Torah Temimah[4] (Epstein, 1989), comments on the Chumash from the last Lubavitcher Rebbe of the 20th century, known simply as The Rebbe[5] (Miller, 2003), and comments on the Chumash from another great sage of the 20th century, Rabbi Joseph B. Soloveitchik, known simple as "The Rav" (Soloveitchik, 2018). Tertiary sources will be referenced herein as appropriate.

Works of biblical leadership have been published previously (Abbe, 2023; N. J. Cohen, 2008; Grumet, 2014; Lapin, 2014; Maxwell John C., 2019; Sacks, 2016, for example) and differ significantly from each other. The work of Rabbi Daniel Lapin is focused on examples of biblical leadership that will lead to spiritual and financial success. The work of Rabbi Lord Jonathan Sacks is based on his decades of experience as Chief Rabbi of the United Kingdom, drawing his insight from questions posed to him and having to look to the Torah for answers, organized into a weekly reader according the parasha[6]. The work of John Maxwell is more of a lesson-based workbook built on

---

[2] "Rashi" is an acronym of his full name, is **Ra**bbi **Sh**lomo Yitzhak**i**
[3] "Ramban" is an acronym of his full name, **Ra**bbi **M**oses **B**en Nahm**an** and is also known as Naḥmanides
[4] The actual name of "Torah Temima" is Rav Baruch HaLevi Epstein
[5] The actual name of "The Rebbe" is Rabbi Menachem Mendel Schneerson
[6] The parasha is the weekly portion of the Torah read in Jewish synagogues

his view as a former Christian clergyman, thus includes the entire "Old Testament" and "New Testament." It is a follow-up of his previous work (Maxwell, 2007) laying out his "irrefutable laws of leadership" based on his personal experience with modern-day secular leaders. The work of Rabbi Elihu Abbe takes the unique approach of taking key leadership attributes like those of John Maxwell and others and looking for support in the Torah. The work of Dr. Norman Cohen focuses on Moshe's growth as a leader, what he himself did to accomplish this self-transformation and looks to secular leaders who demonstrate a particular Mosaic attribute. Finally, the approach of Rabbi Zvi Grumet is to look at the evolution of Moses as a leader, particularly, the transformation of a leader to a leader/teacher; it is organized into five sections of thematically linked topics which in turn are organized into three chapters each, the third of which incorporates the commentary of Jewish sages. The approach in this work is perhaps in some ways most like that of Rabbi Grumet but is unique in that it looks to the Torah first to identify the attributes of a leader. Any known overlap with previous works will be properly noted.

With the number of leaders in the Torah, it may be unclear which one(s) should be used as a reference; the previous works mentioned above use a wide range of personalities. Two Torah verses suggest Moshe[7] (Moses) as the central figure. Looking at Numbers 21:21, it says that "***Israel*** [meaning the Jewish people] sent emissaries

---

[7] In referencing Hebrew words for which there is no English translation, a transliteration of the Hebrew pronunciation will be used; otherwise, the English translation will be used for consistency such as names of people and books of the Bible. Some exceptions will be noted such as the use of Moshe for Moses, Hashem for G-d.

to Sihon." Later in Deuteronomy 02:26, in recapitulating the same story, Moshe says *he himself* sent the messengers. Later, when Moshe's father-in-law joined Israelites after they left Egypt, the Torah says "[Jethro] saw what Hashem had done *for Moshe* and *[for] the people*" (Exodus 18:01). Rashi and Ramban bring that these examples teach us that a generation's leader is like the generation itself. Indeed, several biblical leadership works focus on Moshe (N. J. Cohen, 2008; Grumet, 2014; Soloveitchik, 2013). Since the Torah culminates in being the story of the first generation of Jews, this work will focus on Moshe as the epitome of leadership[8].

One may reasonably ask if it is possible to summarize the type of leadership we expect to find in Moshe. Rabbi Sacks (Sacks, 2016, p.299) would suggest the following: *"...adaptive, getting people to change, persuading them to cease to think and feel like slaves [in their recently redemptive state or future situations] and instead embrace the responsibilities of freedom."* The Rav (Soloveitchik, 2018, commenting on Leviticus 05:04) would suggest the purpose of a leader is to appeal to the good that is in man, to tap into something hidden, his better nature.

---

[8] It is noteworthy that Moses is mentioned at least 58 times (depending on translation) in the New Testament (**https://www.sots.ac.uk/wiki/moses/**) and 136 times in the Quran (**https://en.wikipedia.org/wiki/Moses_in_Islam**)

FRAMING THE LEADERSHIP OPPORTUNITY

When Moshe saw two of the elders (Eldad and Medad) prophesizing seemingly inappropriately (Numbers 11:26) his reaction was much different from when Korah tried to lead a rebellious insurrection against Moshe's leadership (Numbers 16). Moshe understood that Korach was seeking **power** which is divisive whereas Eldad and Medad were wanting to share **influence** which is inclusive. Thus, we see from the Torah that there are different manners in which to lead, via power or via influence. As we shall see from Moshe's example, the preference is to lead by influence. Indeed, as pointed out by Rabbi Sacks (Sacks, 2016, p. 194),

"Not all of us have power, but all have influence, so each can be a leader"

Having stated this, Rabbis Sacks (Sacks, 2016, pp. 102-103) makes the point that leadership is never confined to one role or class. This is supported by Deuteronomy 17:09 where it states that the tribe of Levi had a special role in the Holy Temple. Rabbi Sacks contrasts this to the role of the prophet who is a social critic; a similar point is made by The Rav on Exodus 39:02 (Soloveitchik, 2018).

*Becoming a leade*r is analogous to *new product development* in the business world (Towler, 2022), the future leader being the *product*. This being the case, before initiating "production," a *Value Proposition* would be in order; that is, what *value* our product (the future leader) might offer to those (s)he might lead, in whatever capacity that might be. Using the same *new product development* analogy, it would be expected that a *Target Product Profile* would be the subsequent logical step; that is, what is the profile, or characteristics, of a good leader. Only at this juncture would one define the strategy/path to realize that profile, to become that person; i.e., a training plan.

THE VALUE PROPOSITION (VP)

In the business world and beyond, Vision defines WHY we do what we do at a high level and VP defines the value we will bring among certain attributes. These concepts are closely related. In fact, the VP is derived from the Vision. For example, the vision of a biotech may be to focus on therapies that help those with rare disease. Thus, any proposed product would fit into this vision but would have its own VP for the target population, such as regarding efficacy or safety. In our case, the Vision and VP could perhaps be considered interchangeable.

In Exodus 03:02-04, the narrative describes Moshe at the burning bush as "seeing" the marvelous site. Dr. Cohen points out that Moshe was "seeing" not only the present but the potential on the long-term (N. J. Cohen, 2008, p. 25). This was a deliberate effort. As Dr. Cohen points out later (N. J. Cohen, 2008, p. 29), after Pharoah's immediate rejection of Moshe's request to let the Israelites go, he made sure he was clear on the Vision/mission. In the last book of the Torah, on parasha Re'eh (which is the command, "see," Deut 11:26), The Rebbe points out that the highest level of "seeing" is to be aware of the vision, of what it all means both in the present and future. In Numbers 07:84, after having listed the contributions of each tribe to the newly constructed Tabernacle, Moshe returns to summarize the total. The Rav suggests that Moshe is emphasizing that as important as the individual acts may be, the key is how they contribute to the Vision, the big picture (Soloveitchik, 2018). Thus, understanding the full context of the Vision, both present and future, and keeping it in the forefront is essential for the leader.

It is imperative to understand that repeating a Vision may be considered "prophetic" but in and of itself is not leadership (Grumet, 2014, p.22). Indeed, transformational leaders must "articulate and be committed to the Vision…but never forget the…people whose lives will be transformed" (Grumet, 2014, p.94); i.e., leadership is translating the Vision. The Rav takes this one step further by emphasizing that any leader is a partner with whoever is setting the Vision (Soloveitchik, 2021, on Exodus 10:01) which is predicated on the leader's understanding the Vision to the greatest degree possible (Soloveitchik, 2018, on Exodus 13:13).

As both Dr. Cohen (N. J. Cohen, 2008, p. 31 on Exodus 06:12-13) and The Rav[9] (Soloveitchik, 2021, on Exodus 03:08) point out, Moshe is clear that there are two parts to the vision/mission: 1) Physical Freedom (from servitude); 2) Spiritual Freedom (from Egyptian culture and slave mentality). To achieve either, those being led must comprehend the vision itself. We see the importance of this when Moshe seems to lose his patience for the first time when the Israelites are complaining again about the lack of water (Exodus 17:01-07); Dr. Cohen suggests that this challenge to the ability of the leader reflects their uncertainty in the vision (N. J. Cohen, 2008, p.72). The Rav would likely comment that Moshe is realizing the difficulty of the cultural transformation compared to the simpler redemption

---

[9] The Rav is commenting on Moshe's comment, "I have descended to rescue them from the hand of Egypt," which is the physical freedom.

from slavery (Soloveitchik, 2021, based on Exodus 03:11-12). Later in the narrative, it seems clear that Moshe has a better understanding of the vision when he records in Numbers 10:11-12 that, "the Israelites set out on their journey" and says to his father-in-law that they are "journeying." The Rav points out the significance of the use of the singular "journey" despite the many journeys was that Moshe understood it was all part of the one big picture (Soloveitchik, 2013, p. 169). Finally, with an understanding of the vision intact, one is naturally led to discussion of the VP as stated above, and how the vision will lead to a positive influence on ones' (spiritual) self and the world at large.

Much of a biblical VP is brought down by Rabbi Sacks (Sacks, 2016). In the intro to Rabbis Sacks' work, Ronald Heifetz writes that leadership should **generate capacity**, not dependency, which is in line with his premise that we strive to be (and choose) **adaptive leaders**[10] vs reactive leaders; implicit in this is that **leaders create leaders**. Early in Rabbi Sacks' work (p. 10), he brings that one of the values a biblical leader brings is to **focus on possibility** rather than probability, leading him to be **a person of action**. In Deuteronomy 34:01 Moshe "…went up from the plains of Moab…to the top of the summit…" The Rav brings that this seemingly benign verse is to emphasize that one can be the subject or the object. The mountain climber is the subject using his energy against the forces around him rather than be subservient to his environment (Soloveitchik, 2018). Finally, as his

---

[10] Reactive leaders are emotionally driven, adaptive are driven by principle (Sacks, 2016)

insightful take-home biblical message on how to be a leader Rabbi Sacks beautifully states (p. 286),

*"All you need to do is to write your chapter in the story, do deeds that **heal some of the pain of this world**[11], and act so that **others become a little better for having known you**"*

From Rabbis Sacks, if we are looking to Moshe for the VP, it may be logical to look at his final departing words to the Israelites for insight (i.e., in the book of Deuteronomy). According to Rabbi Sacks (p. 242, p. 276), only here is Moshe defining the key questions of who the Israelites are, what is their task, *why* they (and all leaders) are here. This is the revelation to Israel (and all leaders) to **be teachers/leaders** themselves, to **help people grow** (p. 294) and that "Hashem is not there to relieve you of responsibility [i.e., your mission] but is calling you to it". The large part of the preceding narrative (Genesis, Exodus, Leviticus, Numbers) is a historical reference for future generations. Thus, looking to specific verses in Deuteronomy, we gain further insight into a biblical VP.

In Deuteronomy 01:13, Moshe reminds the Israelites to pick futures leaders from men who are **wise** and **understanding**. Rashi comments that one who is wise does business when he has it and one who is understanding looks for business when there is none. Thus, it seems **reactive action (wisdom)** and **proactive action (understanding)** are key elements of a biblical VP[12]. Ramban

---

[11] In the Jewish vernacular, Tikun Olam, healing the world.

[12] It is important to note that *reactive action* is not the same as a *reactive leader* in that *reactive action* can come from a **reactive leader** or *adaptive leader* as defined above.

suggests this is even more important in higher levels of leadership such as judges.

In Exodus 17: 08-16, the Israelites are fighting an unprovoked, evil attack from the Amalekites. The instruction by Moshe to never forget what the Amalekites did symbolizes that removal of evil is an integral part of the vision (N. J. Cohen, 2008, p. 87); to this day, active remembrance is a deliberate part of Jewish practice. In Deuteronomy 12:02, Moshe is talking about eradicating bad inclinations. In speaking about idols, he says "destroy, you shall destroy." Rashi brings that this seemingly superfluous repetition is to make the point to not only eradicate the action but also to eradicate the root thought (this idea is brought directly in Talmud[13], Tractate Avodah Zarah [idol worship] 45b). Thus, **eradication of roots of idol worship specifically and negativity in general** in this world may also be part of VP.

In Deuteronomy 12:12-13, Moshe lays out what will happen in the future, from the Israelite's time in the desert to the ultimate height of spirituality during the establishment of the Holy Temple. This is a period of 479 years, centuries beyond Moshe's own lifetime. While most individuals may not need to plan that far ahead, is does give the template that **long-term planning** (creating a legacy) is appropriate to include in the VP.

---

[13] The Talmud is a collection of writings that covers the full gamut of Jewish law and tradition, compiled, and edited between the third and sixth centuries CE. Written in a mixture of Hebrew and Aramaic, it records the teachings and discussions of the great academies of the Holy Land and Babylonia. It is organized into "tractates" or topics)

In short, it seems that the VP of a biblical-based leader includes, *but is not limited to*:

1. Generating capacity vs dependency
2. Being adaptive to the needs of the people
3. Focusing on possibilities
4. Being a person of action, both
   a. reactive action (wisdom) and
   b. proactive action (understanding)
5. Eradicating of roots of idol worship specifically, and of negativity in general
6. Providing long-term planning for continued success

THE "TARGET PRODUCT PROFILE" OF A LEADER

General comments

In drug development, once one establishes the Value Proposition (e.g., the future treatment will provide a more efficacious and safer option than that currently available), one moves to define the detailed attributes that deliver this value, the so-called Target Product Profile (TPP). Given the VP of a biblically-based leader has been established above, we are now ready to explore the TPP of the future leader, elucidated below according the various attributes espoused by Moshe.

The attributes chosen on which to expand have been selected somewhat arbitrarily, as they are encountered in the Torah, and then arranged according to the author's thinking. This is by no means the only way to organize these ideas, nor should it be understood as the final word on possible attributes. Lastly, it should not be surprising that of the examples that follow, some will seemingly fit in more than one category, or even categories not listed.

Accountability

Copied under license from https://www.vecteezy.com

Accountability is an attribute both for the leader as well as those (s)he leads. Not only does the leader need to be held accountable, (s)he must also hold those led accountable. Examples of both follow.

We see that Moshe as a leader himself is held to account. In Exodus 32:07, Moshe is receiving the details of the mission (i.e. the Torah) from Hashem on Mount Sinai. Meanwhile, his Israelite followers below have grown impatient with the seemingly extended delay and have built a golden calf to worship. Hashem, knowing this has occurred, says to Moshe, "Go, *descend*, for your nation that you brought up from the land of Egypt has acted corruptly." On this verse, The Rav (Soloveitchik, 2018) agrees with Rashi saying that "Go, descend" means that Moshe is being demoted, so to speak. He was only given his position because of the people and is accountable if they are not following; i.e., a leader without followers is not a leader. Dr. Cohen adds that the phrase *"your nation/people"* is an indication of Moshe's being held accountable as well (N. J. Cohen, 2008, p. 113). We see this idea again in Leviticus 09:04 where it says, "…today the

Lord is appearing *to you* (2nd person plural in Hebrew, אֲלֵיכֶם). The Rav points out that the significance of the 2nd person plural is to emphasize that the Israelites' audience with Hashem is tied to Moshe, since He always appeared only to Moshe in 1st person singular. In other words, a leader is accountable for the successes and failures of those being led and must realize one's destiny demands the ability to suffer disapproval and anguish at the hand of, and because of, the masses (Soloveitchik, 2018, p. 83). The Rav makes the additional point that this was the first serious defeat for Moshe and at this point his accountability changed from that of a redeemer to that of a king (Soloveitchik, 2013, pp. 160-161).

The first example of Moshe's holding himself (or being held) accountable is in Exodus 04:21 where Hashem says to Moshe, "When you go to return to Egypt, *see* all the signs that I have placed in your hand…." To this verse, Ramban brings that "*see*" is in reference to Moshe's staff, that he is to execute the plan and is *accountable*. A second, later example comes from Exodus 13:19, " Moses took Joseph's bones with him, for he [Joseph] had adjured the sons of Israel, saying, God will surely remember you, and you shall bring up my bones from here with you" (sic). The Rav teaches the significance of this comes from the fact that Moshe is the grandson of Levi, one of the biggest antagonists to Joseph and his dreams of rising above his older brother and even his father[14] (Soloveitchik, 2008). Moshe was holding himself accountable for agreements that preceded him. Yet another comes from Exodus 16:03 where the Israelites have just been

---

[14] See Genesis 37 for complete story of Joseph's dreams

redeemed from slavery and are complaining to Moshe at Elim because they only have water and dates (the manna from the sky has not yet begun). Rabbi Grumet brings that from his response he feels in some way accountable for this situation, even though he neither created it nor can directly change it (Grumet, 2014, p.71). Yet another example comes from Exodus 32:32 where Hashem tells Moshe that he is considering killing off the Israelites for the sin of the golden calf and restarting with Moshe to build a new nation. To this Moshe replies that if that is the case, he does not want to be in the Torah. Ramban brings that Moshe did not want it to be said that he was not worthy to speak for them; he wanted to be held *accountable*.

When a subset of the Jews sinned by making a golden calf, Moshe goes to Hashem to asks for forgiveness (Exodus 32:27, 30). The need for forgiveness was not only for those who were actively involved in the worship of the idol but also for the others not stopping them. That Moshe felt he himself needed to ask Hashem for forgiveness shows the "buck stops with him," that he is holding himself *accountable* but also alludes to the *accountability* of the congregation. A very personal instance comes from Numbers 25 where the people committed the sin of adultery and idol worship with the daughters of Moab at which Moshe broke down and cried, having realized his students were not living up to his expectations; his distraught nature was an indication of his holding himself accountable (Soloveitchik, 2018). A final example comes from Numbers 27:01-07, where Tzelophedad's daughters complain to Moshe that, since their father is dead and they have no brothers, they will not be entitled to any property in the promised land, but believe they should. Rabbi

Grumet points out that although the answer to the question seems to have evaded Moshe, he still held himself accountable and advocated on their behalf (Grumet, 2014, p.90)

As a transition to holding others accountable, we can use the same verses just mentioned above (Exodus 32:27, 30). In addition to petitioning Hashem for forgiveness due to sin of the golden calf, Moshe also commands those who did not sin to kill those who did. Ramban and Rashi both concur that this was an emergency that called for drastic action, but even then, the punishment was limited to those who were worshipping the calf by sacrificing to it.

Finally, in Moshe's farewell to the people, he provides guidance on accountability after he is gone. In Deuteronomy 11:26, the Israelites are told, "see today I present before you a blessing and a curse." The blessing is to be received if the law is followed and the curse if it is not followed. The phrasing of this immediately sets up a system of *accountability*, of what will transpire if one acts one way or another. It also fits the criterium that every conditional agreement lays out at least two possible outcomes. Some verses later (Deut. 29:9), Moshe is instructing Israelites that when he is gone, they must "stand firm" (Nitzavim, נִצָּבִים) with the instructions they have been given after which he instructs (in Deuteronomy 29:28) "...the revealed things apply to us and our children..." On this verse The Rav explains that the message is that there is a shared accountability to ensure a lasting understanding of the mission (Soloveitchik, 2018). A few verses later (30:11) Moshe tells the Israelites, that "it (the Torah, their mission) is not in the skies;" it is in their reach and they must choose for it to live or die. In fact, in Deuteronomy 33:04, the narrative states directly, "The Torah that Moses commanded us is a *legacy*..." From these examples, we see Moshe is telling the Israelites they themselves will be held accountable.

Thus, we see that accountability is not only for oneself, but also for the people being led and even for those who come later. Significantly, this can include making difficult decisions, such as issuing a death sentence or alluding to a consequence that could occur later. Indeed, Rabbi Grumet considers strict adherence to the value/principles alluded to in the Vision (which manifests itself in making difficult decision) as one of the two pillars of leadership (Grumet, 2014, p102). In summary, creating a legacy of accountability is critical for a leader.

Being a person of honor

Copied under license from https://www.vecteezy.com

Today's society often excuses the peccadillos of leaders (both secular and religious) by saying that they are "only human." One of the lessons we learn from Moshe is that leaders should be held to a higher standard. From a biblical perspective, a leader should be a person of honor. Like accountability, this applies not only to the leader but needs to be instilled in the followers as well.

In Exodus 18:15 it says that Moshe's father-in-law, Jethro, came to him in the "wilderness" (desert). The significance of specifying "in the wilderness" is to show the honor accorded Moshe by Jethro, who himself was a high priest of Midian and perhaps the father of modern-day Druze[15]. Jethro was coming from his comfortable home to this desolate place to visit his son-in-law. This act in and of itself speaks to the high regard for Moshe held by a high-ranking non-Israelite, a model to be emulated. Another interesting example comes from Exodus 32:01 where the Israelites famously ask Aaron to make a G-d for them because they believe Moshe has

---

[15] https://en.wikipedia.org/wiki/Druze

disappeared. Rabbi Grumet points out that this otherwise despicable request ironically speaks to the honor with which the people held Moshe (Grumet, 2014, p. 177).

One may ask how Moshe came to deserve such honor. An old mentor of mine would say, "provide value and you will be valued." One could extrapolate this to, "act honorably and you will be honored." The next question would be about where Moshe demonstrates honorable behavior. Rabbi Abbe (Abbe, 2023, p. 222) cites Exodus 35:05-19 as one example. In this instance, Moshe is asking for donations to build the tabernacle in the desert. Rabbi Abbe brings that when Moshe was collecting money, he wore a garment with no hem to ensure there was no suspicion that he might be embezzling any money. Rabbi Abbe correlates this with Covey's principle of "trust" (Covey, 1989). Lest one suspect this was simply Moshe's nature, we see from Numbers 16:15 after Korach rebels that a distressed Moshe complains to Hashem saying that he has not wronged the people or even taken a single donkey, even though Rashi contends he rightfully would be entitled. Rabbi Grumet points out that the trust (and honor) the Israelites came to have for Moshe did not come immediately but evolved in Exodus 04-14, over 10 chapters[16] (Grumet, 2014, p. 170). In Numbers 07:1-8, Moshe has just erected the desert Tabernacle and collected gifts from each of the tribes, but interestingly lists each set of gifts even though they were exactly the same. On this

---

[16] In Exodus 04:01, Moshe declares, "they [the Israelites] will not trust me" to redeem them from Egypt; in Exodus 04:31 Moshe confirms that the Israelites do not believe he is there to lead them; in Exodus 14:31 when they are finally being led out of Egypt, the narrative reads they "trusted in the Lord and Moshe his servant."

act, The Rav brings that he was showing honor to each tribe by both acknowledging the gifts themselves and the unique intentions of the individual tribes (Soloveitchik, 2018). Thus, we see Moshe is deliberate regarding his actions to ensure it garners the trust and honor of his followers.

Not only is honorability an attribute for the leader, but one to be taught to the people as well. One example comes from Deuteronomy (16:18, 20) which begins the weekly parasha of Shoftim (Shoftim means judges in Hebrew). In these verses, Moshe lays out the proper behavior for Judges. In particular, he says they must act honorably and be careful not to pervert judgement by: 1) Not noting a person's position, 2) Not taking a bribe, even if to ensure they judge fairly, 3) Pursuing righteousness, ensuring the most learned person is selected as a judge or guide.

Thus, we see from Moshe's example that being a person of honor is realized in three ways: 1) demonstrating you are honorable; 2) being recognized by others as honorable; 3) teaching followers by both example and lessons to act honorably

Challenging authority

Copied under license from https://www.vecteezy.com

Having the "right" to challenge authority, not to mention the "chutzpah"[17] to do so requires a certain degree of character. It is perhaps appropriate, then, that this topic follows the topic of honor. Only a person of honor would have such a "right" to act so brazenly as to directly challenge authority, and know how to do so in an appropriate manner, and at an appropriate time. A few examples follow.

When Moshe asks Hashem what he should tell the enslaved Israelites is His name, Hashem instructs Moshes to tell them His name is, "I will be that I will be"[18] (Exodus 03:14). Rashi says that this alludes to the current subjugation under the Egyptians as well as future ones under other nations. However, Moshe recognized how demoralizing this could be to tell the Israelites he is coming on behalf of Hashem to redeem them so that he can redeem them again later. When Moshe relates this to the Israelites, he only repeats the first part of the phrase, I will be. Thus, Moshe challenged the highest authority

---

[17] Chutzpah is Jewish vernacular for "nerve"
[18] Note this is often mistranslated as "I am that I am" which is not only incorrect, it also would not make sense given the sage Rashi's commentary

in this example knowing this was the right thing to do at this time. This would not be the last time Moshe "challenges" Hashem or other authority.

In Exodus 08:16, Moshe is commanded to "arise early in the morning and stand before Pharoah" but is not told the details on how to perform this act. The Rav comments that Moshe always met Pharoah at the Nile because it was a symbol of Egyptian power. He further makes note from the wording that Moshe was not "petitioning" Pharoah, but demanding (Soloveitchik, 2008). Moshe knew that a direct challenge to the most powerful man in the world was needed at this juncture.

When Moshe was on the top of Mount Sinai receiving the law, he asked to see the glory of Hashem (Exodus 33:18). At face value, this seems very "chutzpadik," to ask the highest authority to share his secrets. Rashi brings that the timing is noteworthy in that it was not appropriate before now. However, now Moshe and the Israelites are at the pinnacle of spirituality, receiving the holy law, making this a most appropriate time. Rabbi Abbe (Abbe, 2023 p. 179) correlates this with Dale Carnegie's principle of "persuasion"(Carnegie, 2022). Thus, we see Moshe had an acute sense of timing.

One of the most well-known stories from the text is that of the "golden calf." While Moshe is on Mt. Sinai receiving the Torah (Exodus 32), the Israelites below grew impatient and built an idol, a golden calf, violating one of the core tenets of their mission, provoking Hashem to destroy the nation and start anew with Moshe. Dr. Cohen points out that Moshe argues vociferously against this idea. First, he throws Hashem's own word back on him pointing out that they were "my [Hashem's] people" back in Exodus 07:14 but only now are they "your [Moshe's] people," now that they have committed a grave sin. Moshe also goes so far as to cast some blame on Hashem himself, for leaving them so long in Egypt, a land of idolatry after having placed them there in the first place (N. J. Cohen, 2008, pp. 115-116).

The final example in this category occurs when the spies came back from scouting out Canaan for the pending conquest. To their discredit, most (8 of the 10) gave an unnecessarily bad report to dissuade the Israelites which ultimately led to the 40 years of wandering in the desert. Hashem was "frustrated" at this lack of faith after all they had seen. In response, Hashem told Moshe he would annihilate the Israelites and rebuild the nation from Moshe himself (Numbers 14:13). Moshe has the audacity to challenge this decision. Moshe uses the logic that it might appear that Hashem could not defeat the Canaanites and that was the reason for destroying his fledgling nation. As pointed out by both Rashi and Ramban, Moshe does this even though it would have been easier for Moshe to go along with the plan. Torah Temimah goes further in pointing out the syntax in Moshe's argument is such that it suggests Hashem would look weak like a woman[19]. Thus, we see that challenging authority often takes courage, a risk to oneself and requires a sense of timing.

We see from these examples that challenging authority, even the highest authority is an attribute of a true leader. One may ask if the

---

[19] This phraseology should be judged in the context of society at the time and not modern sensibilities

courage it takes to challenge a leadership is inherent in "natural born leader" or something learned along the way. We can see from Moshe's sister Miriam's refusing to obey Pharoah and kill the male babies (Exodus 01:07), that this is indeed a trait that ran in his family, so being surrounded by leaders certainly helps. But we see more clearly from Moshe who shows there is an appropriate time and an appropriate manner (i.e., with logical arguments).

Delegation

"Delegation" by Shayna Rochel Towler (2024)

Delegation may understandably be thought of as simply instructing others to do work, whatever the motivation might be. From Moshe, we see delegation itself is more complex than it may seem. To begin with, there are multiple reasons to delegate and it does not completely remove all accountability from the delegator. Secondly, not only is there the act of delegating but also accepting delegation. Finally, there is a proper way to delegate

Realizing one's limitations

When Moshe inducts his brother Aaron to be the high priest which designates him and only him as high priest, the only one to perform certain sacrifices (Leviticus 08:23), there is a special cantillation symbol called a "shalshelet" over the word for "he sacrificed"

(וַיִּשָּׁטֵט)[20]. Rabbi Sacks (Sacks, 2016, p. 131) brings that the symbol indicates an internal struggle. He explains the struggle was Moshe realizing that as leader he cannot do it all. In Leviticus 09:22, Aaron, as one of the appointed priests, blesses the Israelites. The Rav notes that priests alone were given this role and Moshe could not participate, even though Aaron was his brother and they were from the same tribe (Soloveitchik, 2018). Thus, delegation is a necessity and a natural part of being a leader.

Delegation serves both delegate and delegator

One may reasonably ask if the delegate is simply a task-master for the leader. We see an answer to this from when Moshe delegates to Betzalel to first build the ark to hold the stone tablets, then the sacred vessels and finally the tabernacle (Ex. 31:71). Betzalel argues that the order should be reversed to which Moshe agrees. Later in the narrative, as the Israelites are defending themselves against the unprovoked attack from the Amalekites, Moshe's precise wording to Joshua to "choose men and go and do battle" not only relieves Moshe of the responsibility but shows his trust in his successor (N. J. Cohen, 2008, p. 81). One can see from these examples that delegation also means giving stewardship, lifting those to whom responsibility is given. Indeed, Rabbi Sacks (Sacks, 2016, p. 93) points out that inserting the construction of the Tabernacle at this place in the narrative makes Betzalel and the Israelites co-architects of their own

---

[20] The Shalshelet (Hebrew: שלשלת) is a cantillation mark found in the Torah that designate to the designated reader on the Sabbath to "sing" the word. It is one of the rarest used, occurring just four times in the entire Torah, in Genesis 19:16, Genesis 24:12, and Genesis 39:08, and in Leviticus 08:23.

destiny. Although perhaps not directly related to delegation per se, Rabbi Abbe (Abbe, 2023, p. 74) correlates this with Covey's principle of "first things first" (Covey, 1989). Thus, we see delegation serves not only the one delegating but also those to whom a responsibility is given.

Delegation as internal or external idea

The insight into the need to delegate may initiate not only from the leader himself but also from others. Indeed, after the giving of the Torah, Jethro saw that Moses was overwhelmed with the questions and legal struggles being brought to him by the Israelites (Exodus 18:19). Jethro's suggestion was that Moshe set up lower courts and even went so far as to tell Moshe he should ask Hashem about this; Moshe humbly accepts and acts on it right away.

In the previous example of Moshe's delegation to Betzalel, Ramban brings from Gemara (Brachos 55a) that Moshe also "discussed" this with Hashem. Later in the narrative (Exodus 36:02), Moshe goes on to say that those who are similarly endowed with wisdom and whose heart inspired them to be appointed should volunteer as delegates. Taken together, this speaks not only to the fact that the impetus to delegate may come from outside but also to the correctness of conferring with others on the appropriateness of any delegation.

Delegation as a means of establishing connectivity

Delegation may not only be due to inability/capacity to do the work. When the Israelites were complaining because they had become dissatisfied with just manna, the wrath of Hashem flared

(Numbers 11:12, 14). Moshe tells Hashem that his leadership role had become too heavy. Ramban brings that Moshe recognized that he needs other leaders (the elders) to share in the burden. The Rebbe brings a particularly insightful comment that Moshe recognized he could not completely empathize with the complaints of the people, presumably because of his higher level, so would need to delegate to those who could. Indeed, when Moses first came down from the mountain after having received the Torah, the people were scared to approach him (Exodus 34:31). Rashi comments that Moshe first called the heads of the tribes (Ramban is of the opinion he called the princes) to establish a deeper connection with them first. Thus, even a relationship can be "delegated" (It is noted that this could also fit into other attributes such as "Establishing a legacy," "Empathy" or even others not mentioned here)

Holding the delegate accountable

Once the realization of the need to delegate is made, it is not as simple as assigning a task or role. Immediately following Moshe's realization of his own emotional limits, he gathers and appoints 70 elders to help share the burden of leadership (Numbers 11:17). Dr. Cohen brings that this shows that Moshe as a leader trusts those to whom a task has been delegated (N. J. Cohen, 2008, p. 90). Rashi brings that the elders had to be made aware explicitly of the troublesome nature of the Israelites. Rabbi Abbe (Abbe, 2023, p. 279) correlates this behavior with Willet's principle of "navigating a challenge"(Willet, 2016). Thus, we see that the delegate must know that (s)he is trusted and fully aware of the role to which (s)he is being appointed, or else (s)he could not be held fully accountable in his/her new role.

Lifting delegates to the role

In addition to the importance of the delegates' being completely informed of the role, they may need reassurance to accept the position. As soon as Moshe appoints Aaron to be the high priest, we see that Moshe had to "encourage" him to approach the altar (Leviticus 09:07). Rashi states that Aaron was insecure about his new role (perhaps because of his participation in the sin of the golden calf) so Moshe had to "lift him up" by telling him "…this is your role, you were chosen." Rabbi Abbe (Abbe, 2023, p. 281) cites this as an example of Willet's principle of "Challenges of leadership."(Willet, 2016). Thus, we see that delegation is not a "once-and-done," but likely requires help from the leader to lift the individuals to their respective new roles.

Method for selecting delegates

One may now wonder what are the general "job requirements" for a leader to consider when choosing delegates. In selecting the 70 elders as Moshe did to share in leadership (Numbers 11:17), one can assume there certainly must have been some criteria beyond simply being an elder. Dr. Cohen suggests we see the criteria from when Moshe selected men for lower courts (Exodus 18:21) where he chose "…men of substance [strong], God fearers [understanding of vision], men of truth [honorable], who hate monetary gain [non-materialistic]…" (N. J. Cohen, 2008, p. 93). The specific criteria of truthfulness may be learned from Moshe trying to convince Jethro to stay with the Israelites in the desert rather than return to Midian

(Numbers 10:31)[21]. The Hebrew reads you "*were* eyes for us" but the first century translator, Onkelos[22], writes this as "*will be* eyes for us." On this Rashi comments that Moshe recognizes that Jethro provided objective, honest insight and enlightenment on truths that may not otherwise be appreciated. Thus, we learn from Moshe that delegates must be chosen carefully among these criteria.

Delegation as a mechanism for driving unity

Finally, Rabbi Lapin (Lapin, 2014) suggests that inherent to delegation is specialization. For example, before ascending Mount Sinai to receive the Torah, Moshe spends 29 verses blessing the individual tribes, as opposed to just blessing everyone at once (Deuteronomy 33:06-34). Rabbi Lapin suggests (p. 166) the implication is that Moshe was stressing that part of delegation is specialization. Indeed, Rabbi Sacks (Sacks, 2016, pp. 102-103) makes note of Deuteronomy 17:09 where Moshe assigns specific tasks to the tribe of Levi in the Holy Temple and contrasts this to the role of a prophet who is a social critic. Rabbi Sacks argues that delegation should make clear that leadership is never confined to one role or class. As Rabbi Lapin contends, specialization (diversity of roles) drives unity through interdependence. Indeed, The Rav brings from Numbers 32:33 (when Moshe splits the tribe of Menashe to be on both

---

[21] Whether Jethro did stay with the Israelites or not is the subject of some debate but there is ample evidence he did at least end up in Canaan. The "Tomb of Jethro" (also known as Nebi Shu'eib, Nabi Shu'ayb or Neby Shoaib), located adjacent to the abandoned Muslim village of Hittin near Tiberias, has been administered by Druze authorities since 1948

[22] Onkelos is possibly identical to Aquila of Sinope, who was a Roman national who converted to Judaism in Tannaic times (c. 35–120 CE). He is the author of the Targum Onkelos (c. 110 CE) which is included in every Jewish Bible.

sides of the Jordan river) that each half of the tribe would be performing a slightly different role which in the end would ensure communication and unity across the Jordan (Soloveitchik, 2018). The Rav adds (as a comment to Deuteronomy 14:01) that it was not just that the Israelites as followers of Moshe were destined to a common fate based on their mission but rather a collection of individuals dependent on each other to succeed (*ibid.*). Thus, delegation drives specialization which in turns drives unity.

Derech Eretz ("correct conduct")

Copied under license from https://www.vecteezy.com

Ethics of our forefathers

It has been asked many times why the Torah has such a long narrative preceding the giving of the Torah at Mount Sinai, the moment Israelites become the Jewish nation. One answer given is that the book of Genesis is a description of the ethics of the forefathers which are inherited by Moshe. The Torah uses the narrative to set limits on what is acceptable and what is not. The ascent of Moshe represents the culmination of the morals and ethics based on the previous 20 generations. What then is the proper conduct as exemplified by Moshe?

On being a mensch[23],

We must begin this discussion by clarifying that proper conduct is not only the leader themselves determining what type of individual to become, but also what is wanted from those being led (the future leaders). In Deuteronomy 12:10, Moshe instructs the Israelites

---

[23] Mensch is a Yiddish word meaning a person of honor and integrity

regarding the correct manner in which to bring a sacrifice to Hashem. In this part of the narrative, Moshe is teaching that the sacrifice should be of the choicest possibilities, indicating that one must always strive to do the very best, not just the minimum. This concept is clearly meant be extrapolated to all behavior. For example, in Numbers 27:16-17, Moshe says to the Israelites, "May the Lord, G-d of all spirits, choose a man, who will bring them out and lead them in." On the use of the word, "man," Rabbi Sacks (Sacks, 2016, p. 222) points out that this is not reference to gender but rather to someone who is a mensch, one of impeccable conduct. But, what do we learn from Moshe himself?

Leading from the front

One aspect of proper conduct of a leader is their "position in the pack." A common image used to depict leadership in the business world has been the famous photograph of a pack of wolves traveling through deep snow. This image has been used to describe a leader using many popular terms based on a misinterpretation of the true nature of the picture; everything from the leader's being in the middle to the leader's being in the rear. As described by the International Wolf Center, the leader(s) are clearly those in front[24]. Of course, we are not wolves. Nonetheless, Rabbi Sacks (Sacks, 2016, p. 222) brings from the same verse cited above (Numbers 27:16-17), "bringing them out and bringing them in" indicates that a leader must be *in front* but not so much that when they turn around there is no one there. (This

---

[24] See https://wolf.org/headlines/caption-attached-to-photo-of-wolves-traveling-through-snow-as-a-pack-is-false/

also speaks to a certain amount of empathy and understanding of diversity which we cover separately). While this is a physical description of the attribute *"correct conduct,"* perhaps the more intangible aspects are even more noteworthy.

Daring to be different

One intangible attribute of correct conduct is recognizing that the normative behavior in which one finds oneself may not be worth emulating. This was certainly the case at the birth of the Jewish nation, where idol worship and even human sacrifice were common. In Deuteronomy 12:23, Moshe tells the Israelites to "be strong in their commitment" not to eat blood. The significance of this was that eating blood was quite common at the time. The lesson is to be true to one's values, not to let others influence you and being different is the norm for a leader. Rabbi Sacks (Sacks, 2016, p. 16) explicitly states that a leader shows it is okay to be different, and to refuse to assimilate to the dominant culture or religion.

The power of speech

Expanding further on the aspect of being different from society is controlling one's speech. And why might this be so significant? In Genesis 01:03-27, each act of creation was preceded with "And Hashem said", attesting to the enormous power given to speech. But this is not limited to the Almighty. In Genesis 02:07, it says "He [Hashem] breathed into his [Adam's] nostrils the soul of life, and man became a living soul." According to Onkelos' translation God's breath became a "speaking spirit" in Adam.

Controlling speech

And what do we see from Moshe, our paragon of leadership, on the topic of controlled speech? In the narrative of Numbers 21:31, Rashi brings that Moshe was clearly afraid of doing battle with Og, the Amorite king of Basham, because of any favor Og may have gained from Hashem from helping Abraham (Genesis 14:13). But Moshe did not share this fear with the Israelites. The Rebbe brings that this was because of his recognition of the power of speech and Moshe not wanting to engender fear among the Israelites before battle. And from where did Moshe learn this important lesson? One may assume that this was a characteristic of the forefathers. Rabbis Sacks (Sacks, 2016, pp. 142, 149) suggests that Moshe learned this lesson for himself early during his first encounter with Hashem at the burning bush (Exodus 04:01); there Moshe was punished with "leprosy[25]" when he cast aspersions on the Israelites by suggesting to Hashem that they might not accept him as their redeemer.   Thus, we see that the attribute of controlled speech is of paramount importance. In fact, Rabbi Sacks points out that we can infer from Moshe's experience at the burning bush that not only is speaking badly of someone evil ("lashon hara"[26]), speaking positively is good, lifting the recipient.

---

[25] The affliction given Moshe was "Tzara'at" which is often mistranslated as leprosy. This heavenly-given punishment was for several sins, the most well-known being "evil speech"/ gossiping (**https://aish.com/tzaraat-versus-leprosy/**)

[26] Lashon Hara, literally evil tongue, is used colloquially to refer to gossip but can refer to any type of unnecessary speech, good or evil, which may harm the subject of the speech

Controlled spontaneity

Given the inherently spontaneous nature of lashon hara (gossip), the leader may wonder how to control this attribute and still be a "person of action" as discussed in the VP section above. There is certainly evidence to suggest that "uncontrolled spontaneity" should be avoided. In Numbers 20:02, Miriam has just died and thus the water well that appeared in her merit was no more. In response to the people's complaints about lack of water, Moshe was instructed by Hashem to talk to a rock. Instead, he lost his composure and struck the rock, which ultimately cost him the privilege to enter the promised land. Later, in Leviticus 10:09, Aaron's sons were killed by Hashem for deciding on their own to perform a religious rite in the holy of holies. Rabbis Sacks (Sacks, 2016, p. 137) suggests the wording in the verse (that they brought a "strange fire") can be translated as spontaneous.

The leader as the example

From where did Aaron's sons learn such religious spontaneity mentioned above? One could say from Moshe's striking of the rock, the breaking of the tablets, or other undocumented acts. Rabbi Sacks suggests it was specifically from Moshe's breaking the tablets containing the ten commandments after seeing the Israelites dancing around the golden calf (Exodus 32:15, 19). In any case, uncontrolled spontaneity on the part of a leader can set a dangerous precedence for the followers .

Moshe's impulsive breaking of the tablets may be somewhat surprising given Moshe's visibly demonstrating "controlled spontaneity" earlier in the narrative. When Moshe grows up, he leaves Pharaoh's palace to visit his kin, the Israelites. Seeing an Egyptian beating a Hebrew, Moshe checks to make sure no one is looking, kills the Egyptian, and then buries the body in the sand (Exodus 02:11–12). Rabbi Sacks (Sacks, 2016, p. 4) makes the point that although it was admirable that Moshe was a "person of action," it was even more so that he was controlling his spontaneity. Thus, controlling spontaneity is to be lauded both for the leader's self and the effect it has on others.

Managing perceptions

Being a "person of action" while controlling spontaneity may be seen as part of a more-encompassing attribute of *managing perceptions*. In Numbers 10:31, Moshe is asking his father-in-law Jethro to stay with them and continue to the land of Canaan. Rashi explains the reason is that Jethro himself was a highly regarded person (a priest of Midian) and it might have been thought that his conversion and commitment to this new religion were now being reconsidered, which would lead to a negative *perception* of the overall message of this new movement[27]. Thus, it is important to conduct oneself and instruct others in a way that leave only a desired perception; a leader must be aware of the unconscious messages being sent. To be successful in this struggle, Rabbis Sacks (Sacks, 2016, pp. 211-214) suggests that a leader must surround himself with those who will help in this regard, as Miriam did for Moshe.

---

[27] It seems Moshe was successful as brought by Ramban (referencing Deuteronomy 26:10) and Torah Temimah (referencing Ezekiel 47:23) which indicate Jethro not only brought sacrifices in the new land but was buried there as well, respectively

Leadership servitude

A leadership trait that would naturally bring one to be acutely aware of perception is that of servitude. Although "servant leadership" is a catch phrase in today's management circles, we see this as exemplified by the leader Moshe throughout his adult life. Indeed, Rabbi Abbe (Abbe, 2023, pp. 208-209) correlates the story of Moshe's chasing Jethro's lost sheep and carrying him back to the flock (Exodus 02:02) with Maxwell's principle of "servitude" (Maxwell, 2007). Approximately a year later, when Pharoah finally relented and allowed the Israelites to leave Egypt, Moshe made sure to take the bones of Joseph because of a promise made by his ancestors (Exodus 13:19). Rashi makes the point that a (servant) leader must honor the promises/commitments made before one arrived on the scene. Finally, later in Deuteronomy 04:41, as Moshe is about to die, he establishes the "cities of refuge[28]" for the land of Israel, even though he knows he himself will not enter. Thus, we see that Moshe was the first "servant leader" and established himself as such throughout his life.

Teaching ethics

A final aspect of proper conduct is not only living the life but also *creating the learning opportunity* for those being led. A number of examples exist that we will examine here. Early in the redemption story, Hashem instructs Moshe to have *Aaron* stretch out his hand and turn the waters to blood (Exodus 07:19); the lesson here, says Rashi, is

---

[28] The cities of refuge were six towns in the Land of Israel in which the perpetrators of accidental death (manslaughter) could claim the right of asylum. Outside of these cities, blood vengeance against such perpetrators was allowed by law.

that one must not harm something that was good for you, the Nile having saved Moshe from Pharoah's decree to have all male children killed (Exodus 01:15–22). In Leviticus 10:16-17, Moshe is inquiring of the sons of Aaron (Elazar and Ithamar) about a halachic (legal) issue in front of Aaron. This created the opportunity for the sons to defer to their father as they appropriately did. In Numbers 08:02, Moshe is instructing Aaron how to light the wicks of the candelabra in the Holy Temple, that the wicks should face the "face" (center). Rashi points out the wording here is beha'aloshca (to raise) instead of the more natural behad-lik-cha (to light). The point, explains Rashi, is to teach that Aaron should not move the flame away until it could stay lit on its own, and same with people, to raise others to stand on their own. In Numbers 11:29 Joshua comes to complain to Moshe that Eldad and Medad were prophesizing in the camp instead of joining the other elders with Moshe. Moshe uses this opportunity to correct Joshua on appearing too self-righteous; Ramban brings that Moshe is asking him on whose account is he being a zealot, himself or Moshe. In Moshe's farewell address to the Israelites (Deuteronomy 08:01) Moshe warns the people not to become too prideful about past and pending accomplishments; this is also consistent with his own humility which we have examined above.

Thus, we see that Derech Eretz (correct conduct) is indeed a large aspect of being a leader. It takes many forms, both tangible and intangible.   Some of the more intangible aspects come from having empathy for those being led, which we will explore next.

Empathy and its manifestations

"Empathy" by Shayna Rochel Towler (2024)

A life characterized by completely proper conduct is to be admired and certainly appreciated as an attribute of a true leader. However, without empathy for those being led, one may be destined to be seen as nothing more than a sanctimonious zealot. Sincere empathy becomes evident in concern for those being led which is predicated on intimately knowing them. We see this in Numbers 01:02 where Moshe takes a census of *"the entire assembly…."* On this verse, The Rav suggests the entire assembly is to indicate that Moshe acquainted himself with every individual. This familiarity leads to empathy which in turn manifests itself in various ways, such as manner of speaking and understanding the need for second chances. All this lifts up the followers and allows the future leaders to develop.

Empathy as a basis

Rabbi Grumet holds that compassion (a manifestation of empathy) is one of the two pillars on which leadership is built (Grumet, 2014, p102). The empathy Moshe has for the Israelites is apparent throughout his leadership. Early, in Exodus 02:11, the text is describing Moshe first becoming conscious of the suffering the Israelite slaves. Looking more closely at the text, one learns much about his empathy. For example, it says that Moshe "saw" their [the Israelite's] suffering. Rabbi Abbe (Abbe, 2023, p. 97) cites Rashi, explaining that he set his eyes and heart to feel what they felt. Indeed, The Rav comments that the phrase, "[Moshe] looked at their burdens (וַיַּרְא בְּסִבְלֹתָם)" indicates he experienced it (Soloveitchik, 2018). Dr. Cohen makes the thought-provoking argument that the seemingly superfluous use of the word "brother" in the phrase, "[Moshe] saw an Egyptian beating a Hebrew, *his brother*," indicates the level of empathy he felt (N. J. Cohen, 2008, p. 9); as The Rav would say, they were no longer an "other" but a "thou" (Soloveitchik, 2000). In Exodus 17:01-07, the Israelites are complaining a second time since crossing the sea about the lack of water. Dr. Cohen says that Moshe's passing before the people (verse 5) was to try to understand (empathize) them (N. J. Cohen, 2008, p. 75). In Exodus 18:13, Moshe sat down "to judge the people" to help them resolve their legal questions and understand the pending cultural transformation. The Rav notes the nuance of the Hebrew word "to judge" (לִשְׁפֹּט) which also means to advise, to help, to show concern (Soloveitchik, 2018) which indicates Moshe acted with empathy. Based on yet another linguistic nuance, Dr. Cohen points to Exodus 19:14 where "Moshe came down from the mountain [Mt. Sinai] *to the people* [because they had built an idol]," suggesting that the superfluous phrase "to the people" indicates his desire to understand what was transpiring in order that he might have empathy (N. J. Cohen, 2008, p. 108). In fact, Rabbi Abbe correlates this with Covey's principle of "seek first to understand" (Covey, 1989) which seems to be a prerequisite for empathy

Not long after the revelation at Mount Sinai (Numbers 11:12, 14), the Israelites became dissatisfied with the manna[29] and were complaining, after which the "wrath of Hashem flared". Moshe, in anticipation of the pending punishment, asks Hashem if he is supposed to "carry the people in his bosom" and if so, it is "too heavy." Ramban suggests the motherly reference is because only a mother can feel the pain of pending punishment. Rashi adds that he would rather be killed than see the punishment meted out. What deeper empathy can one expect than this?

In Moshe's last days (Deuteronomy 03:23), he is relating how he asked Hashem to let him go into Canaan. The word he uses is וָאֶתְחַנַּן (entreated). The Rebbe brings that the Gematria[30] of this word is 515, indicating he asked no less than 515 times. One may logically wonder why would he do this since Hashem got angry when he asked. The Rebbe explains that he was not asking for himself but for the people, knowing the great benefit for them if he would accompany them into the land. And finally, in Deuteronomy 10:19, Moshe commands the Israelites, "you shall love the stranger, for you were strangers in the land of Egypt." The Rav points out that the slave experience underlies the very morality and empathy of their new way of life (Soloveitchik,

---

[29] an edible substance which Hashem provided for the Israelites during their travels in the desert during the 40-year period following the Exodus and prior to the conquest of Canaan

[30] a Kabbalistic method of interpreting the Hebrew scriptures by computing the numerical value of words, based on those of their constituent letters.

2018). As the saying goes, sometimes one must "walk a mile in another's shoes" to truly understand and empathize.

The depth of Moshe's connection to the Israelites was apparent throughout his tenure. The question is how it should manifest itself. Dr. Cohen indicates how complex empathy can be by referencing the situation where the Israelites were trapped with their backs to the sea with the Egyptian army closing in (N. J. Cohen, 2008, p. 41). The Israelites fell into groups representing one of four choices:

1. Throw themselves into the sea and hope for the best
2. Give up and return to Egyptian servitude
3. Stand and fight the massive Egyptian army
4. Cry out to Hashem for help

Dr. Cohen suggests that Moshe had to understand (empathize) with each of these groups to successfully move forward. The Rebbe relates a story to illustrate the occasional simplicity of empathy (Jacobson, 2002, p. 200). A woman who approached a venerated rabbi with a tragic situation. He informed her he could not help her but he could cry with her. Complex or simple, we will look how Moshe's empathy manifests itself in two specific behaviors.

Empathy manifested in the manner of speaking

Just as Moshe's empathy is apparent throughout his life as a leader, so is its manifestation into innate concern for those he is leading, which manifests itself in his manner of communication. Two examples have been used earlier in this text. In Exodus 03:14, Moshe asks Hashem what he shall tell the Israelites is His name. Hashem answers, "I shall be that I shall be." But Moshe simply tells the

Israelites that His name is, "I shall be." Rashi brings that the phrase "I shall be that I shall be" indicates Hashem will be with the Israelites during the current Egyptian subjugation and during future subjugations. Moshe shows his empathy by clearly recognizing how disheartening it would be to tell the Israelites that they will come out of this subjugation only to be subjugated again. Later, when Moshe is told he will not be leading the Jews into the promised land, the first thing he is concerned about is who will take over and lead the people. Moshe says, "may the Lord, *G-d of all spirits*, choose a man, who will bring them out and lead them in" (Numbers 27:16-17). Per Rashi, the use of the phrase "*G-d of all spirits*" indicates Moshe's innate empathy for, and understanding of, the diversity of his followers.

Another example of Moshe's empathy manifesting itself in his manner of speaking comes from his last days where he is recounting the travels of the last 40 years. In Deuteronomy 01:01, it begins as "these are the words that Moshe spoke to all Israel." Rashi offers that by phrasing the verse in this way, "these are the words," indicates a vagueness that will follow; Moshe will start listing the places where the Israelites sinned and angered Hashem. Moshe is empathizing by not being too harsh and just alluding to the sin by renaming the place. As one well-known example, Torah Temimah cites the place called Dai Zahav (enough gold) which alludes to the sin of the golden calf. The Rebbe concurs that Moshe's approach is out of respect, to protect the dignity of the people and not mention their sins overtly. Rabbi Abbe (Abbe, 2023, p. 197) correlates this behavior with Carnegie's principle of "constructive criticism." (Carnegie, 2022).

Finally, in Deuteronomy 05:20-28, Moshe is recounting how during the uttering of the ten commandments, the Israelites asked Moshe to listen to the rest because they would die at hearing Hashem's "voice". Although one could make the argument that they should hear all the commandments themselves, this shows Moshe's empathy for the people. Thus, we clearly see that Moshe's manner of speaking (in this example to Hashem himself) was one tangible way in which his empathy for the Israelites was evident.

Empathy manifested in second chances

One of the strongest and most notable examples of Moshe's belief in second chances was after the sin of the golden calf mentioned above. Moshe's word in defense of the Israelites idolatrous sin was, "Why should Your wrath be increased against Your people when You took them out of Egypt" (Exodus 32:11). The Rav makes the point that Moshe was arguing that to reform the formerly pagan ex-slave would take time, that they needed a second chance as a people (Soloveitchik, 2013, p. 213).

In Numbers 09:06-13, the Israelites had recently received the Torah but were spiritually unclean[31] and thus not allowed to bring the sacred Passover sacrifice as commanded. Moshe brings their case to Hashem, and the decision is that they be given a "second chance" (one month later when they are again spiritually clean) to bring the sacrifice; this second Passover ("Pesach Sheini") is observed to varying degrees to this day. Thus, we see from the beginning of

---

[31] A person who touches a corpse becomes spiritually impure

Moshe's role as a leader, he is immediately showing his empathy by allowing for second chances.

Moshe continues his attitude toward second chances throughout the Israelites' 40 years in the desert. In Numbers 32:06 & 18, Moshe chastises the tribes of Gad and Reuven for wanting to stay on the east side of the Jordan because of there being good land for their cattle and not wanting to cross over and conquer Canaan with the rest of the Israelites, the other 10 tribes. Rashi clarifies that the concern was that other tribes might think Gad and Reuven were scared and become demoralized. The Rebbe suggests that Gad and Reuven were not wrong in that they never intended to demoralize the rest of the tribes but they were wrong in not showing empathy for the rest of the tribes. This is what Moshe made them aware of, and why Moshe offered that they would be vindicated if they first helped conquer the land and then returned to the land east of the Jordan. In fact, in Numbers 32:29 Moshe stipulates what will happen to Gad and Reuven if they cross the Jordan and fight and what will happen if not. If they go, they will inherit land in the kingdom of Sihon, but with conditions; in Numbers 32:33, it clarifies that half of the tribe of Menashe[32] will live there as well. Ramban brings that if they chose not to fight, they will be made to fight but would not get an inheritance. Thus, we see that simply offering a second chance is not enough; it must be with conditions. Indeed, Torah Temimah (Epstein, 1989) brings the foundational

---

[32] The Rebbe brings that Zelophehad's daughters (of the tribe of Menashe) who argued for an inheritance despite no male heir to their father showed love for the land which was needed to temper the more materialistic views of Gad and Reuven; for this reason, Menashe was destined to "watch over" Reuven and Gad.

principle from Tractate Kiddushin 61a, that any conditional reward must also have a conditional punishment. Rabbi Abbe (Abbe, 2023, pp. 76-77) equates this with Covey's "win-win" principle (Covey, 1989). Rabbi Sacks (Sacks, 2016, p. 228) also brings this as an example of leadership.

Encouragement

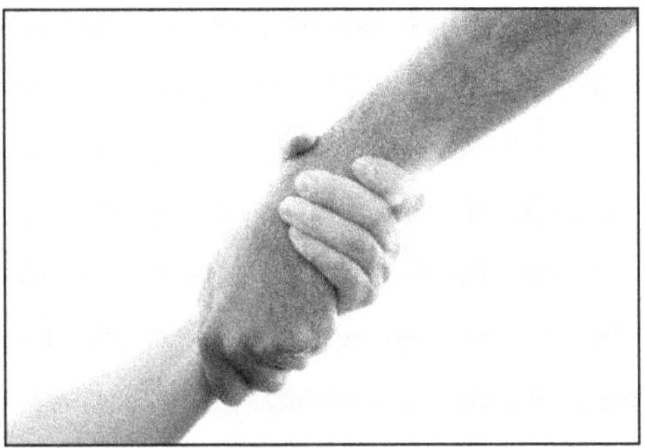

Copied under license from https://www.vecteezy.com

Moshe establishes clearly that a leader must provide encouragement to those around him. In Numbers 01:01-02 the Torah relates one of the times that Moses counts the Israelites, but the phraseology used in the text for "counting" is "lift the head" (שְׂאוּ אֶת־רֹאשׁ). Rabbi Sacks (Sacks, 2016, p. 186) suggests that among the 600,000 or so males, Moshe is lifting the individual heads so they do not feel lost in the crowd. Among the entire congregation he is committed to ensuring they *all* feel encouraged.

A famous story demonstrating the practicality of Moshe's encouragement was during the battle with the Amalekites (Exodus 17:11-12). In this incident, Moshe was watching the battle from a hilltop. If his hands were raised, the Israelites would be winning, if they were lowered, the Amalekites would win. Lest it be thought this success was an open miracle, Rabbi Sacks (Sacks, 2016, pp. 79-80) brings from Mishna Rosh Hoshana 3:8 that this was simply that Moshe was encouraging the Israelites and reminding them to look to heaven and remember their purpose, empowering them to do their job. Dr. Cohen similarly adds that Moshe's role here was encouraging the fighting Israelites to maintain their focus on the long-term purpose, to the broader vision (N. J. Cohen, 2008, p. 83). Dr. Cohen also points to a later place in the narrative where the Israelites were to receive their full mission at the foot of Mount Sinai, where it says Moshe had to lead the people (Exodus 19:17) because they were scared and needed this encouragement from their leader (N. J. Cohen, 2008, p. 100, 104). Thus, the encouragement had a very concrete impact for the Israelites.

Moshe was also committed to providing encouragement for a time when he would not be the leader. As Rabbi Sacks (Sacks, 2016) brings from Exodus 19:06, Moshe tells the people (*and future leaders that will not have the benefit of his presence*) to be a nation of priests. Rabbi Sacks comments these words are the type of encouragement that empower the Israelites to take their destiny into their own hands. Indeed, later in Deuteronomy 30:14, Moshe goes on to tell the Israelites that they will falter in the future but to have *optimism* and *hope* because Hashem will give them a second chance and they will be restored; i.e., it is in their hands. Rabbi Sacks (Sacks, 2016, p. 235) comments here that *optimism* is to believe that things will get better and *hope* is to believe that one can work to make things better; both are forms of encouragement needed from a leader. Moshe is committed to encouraging the Israelites and tells them in Deuteronomy 31:16 to be strong , not lose faith, to move forward and keep improving.

Establishing a legacy

Copied under license from https://www.vecteezy.com

The basic requirements of an established legacy

Many of the attributes discussed thus far are fitting when a leader is around. The question remains what happens when the leader inevitably leaves the role. As pointed out by the late Justice Antonin Scalia (Scalia & Scalia, 2017, p. 85) any good leader is concerned about creating a living legacy, making it necessary to establish a leadership chain that will last for generations to come. By necessity, this must be accompanied by a narrative of the original ideals and even rituals tied to the narrative.

The origin of legacy

Is legacy only from the present? In Deuteronomy 29:13-14, the narrative records the following, "But not only with you am I making this covenant and this oath, but with those standing here with us today before the Lord, our God, and [also] with those who are not here with us, this day." The simple meaning of this is to imply those in the future are part of the vision/legacy. The Rav makes the point that even in the past when Abraham looked toward a future for his offspring, he too was establishing a legacy *from the future* (Soloveitchik, 2008, p. 65). Thus, the vision/mission is not just something communicated from today to the future, but an overall understanding of what could be, making the future responsible for the present (Soloveitchik, 2008, p. 202)

Moshe's concern about future generations

Early in his tenure Moshe expressed deep concern about the future of the Israelites after he was gone. In Exodus 12:26, Moshe speaks to the Israelites of Passover[33] celebrations far in the future, telling the Israelites what to do when "your [future] son asks you what is this [ancient Passover] service to you?" On this Rabbi Grumet comments that Moshe is sparking a long-term national memory, ***a legacy*** (Grumet, 2014, pp.180-181). We also see this concern played out when Moshe set up the lower court system in which "...the difficult cases they would bring to Moshe." (Exodus 18:26). The Rav emphasizes that the difficulty was not measured by monetary measurement but rather the degree of explanation needed for the vision to be a living legacy. (Soloveitchik, 2018).

In his final days Moshe commanded the Israelites, "When you cross [into the promised land], you shall write all the words [of this mission]..." (Deuteronomy 27:03), which is commonly understood to mean that it was written in all the 70 known languages; i.e. a way of

---

[33]Passover is the major Jewish Spring festival which commemorates the liberation of the Israelites from Egyptian slavery, involving a traditional meal and retelling of the exodus from Egypt.

preserving the legacy.   In Deuteronomy 29:13-14, Moshe emphasizes, "it is not only with you I am establishing this covenant but with whoever…is not with us;" i.e., future generations, as emphasized by Rabbi Sacks (Sacks, 2016, p. 283).   The point of this according to The Rav (Soloveitchik, 2018) is that those who come later must see themselves as if they received the mission themselves; this will be a bridge to the future that can withstand personal or cultural antagonism.   Finally, in Deuteronomy 29:9-30:20, Moshe is instructing Israelites that when he is gone, they must "stand firm" and that "it [the Torah, their mission] is not in the skies;" it is in their reach and they must choose (Deuteronomy 30:15) between "life" (i.e. a legacy) or "death" (i.e., disappearance from annals of history).   Rabbi Grumet comments that Moshe's sincere concern on this topic is best understood in light of the fact that he had no interest in establishing a dynasty, a legacy for his and his sons[34], but rather legacy for the vision itself (Grumet, 2014, p208).

Moshe similarly focused on leadership to maintain legacy.   The Rav points to Exodus 17:19, as one such example.   There, Moshe instructs the future leader Joshua to pick men to fight the Amalekites "for us." The Rav suggests that this wording so early in the narrative indicates Moshe seeing Joshua as a future leader. The fact that Moshe inscribed not only his choosing of Joshua but also the success of the battle (Exodus 17:04) further supports this concept of Moshe choosing the legacy leader early (Soloveitchik, 2018).   In his farewell address

---

[34] It is noteworthy that after the brief introduction of Moshe's sons, the disappear into the background

(Deuteronomy 03:26) Moshe tells the Israelites that he is not being allowed to enter Canaan "le-ma-anchem" (לְמַעַנְכֶם) which is usually translated, "because of you" (i.e. your sin of provoking me when you wanted water). Dr. Cohen bring a unique understanding that "le-ma-anchem" can also mean "for your sake," that Moshe's presence would stand in the way of a future leader (N. J. Cohen, 2008, p. 159) In short, for the continuity of the Israelites and their new way of life, a legacy of personal choice and leader must be established and maintained and the current leader must "let go."

Defining the future leader(s)

One of the most important tasks is to define who will continue a seamless chain of leadership, who will and will not become leaders. Rabbi Sacks (Sacks, 2016, p. 100) points out that Moshe's children were not prophets. This speaks to what leadership legacy is not, it is not hereditary. On the other hand, in Deuteronomy 31:7 and Deuteronomy 31:28, Moshe sets up a clear succession plan through Joshua and stresses to him the need to depend on elders. We see from here that depending on elders is part of maintaining a legacy and that we cannot expect one's successor to be a cookie-cutter image of oneself (Moshe did not consult elders but Joshua would need to do so). Rabbi Abbe (Abbe, 2023, p. 28) correlates this with Willet's principle of "challenges of authority" (Willet, 2016), although the connect is not completely clear. Rabbi Sacks (Sacks, 2016, p. 287) insightfully brings, based on Rashi, that the coming times will be different, and the new leader will need to be even more adaptive than Moshe himself, which may explain the emphasis on consulting the elders. Indeed, in the final tractate of the Talmud in a section referred to as Pirkei Avos

(Ethics of our Fathers) it states the Jewish tradition that, "Moses received the Torah at Sinai and transmitted it to Joshua, Joshua to the elders, and the elders to the prophets, and the prophets to the Men of the Great Assembly[35]" thus documenting the legacy through specific leadership.

Moshe clearly took great care in the eventual choice of Joshua as the future leader. In Numbers 27:16-17, Moshe says, " may the Lord, G-d of all spirits, choose a man, who will bring them out and lead them in." Rabbi Sacks (Sacks, 2016, p. 222) points out the use of the word "man" is not a reference to gender but rather to someone who is a mensch[36] (as mentioned elsewhere in this work). Indeed, on Numbers 27:18 where Moshe is commanded, "…take for yourself Joshua…," The Rav stresses that Joshua was chosen not because of his innate ability but because of his dedication and loyalty to Moshe and the Vision (Soloveitchik, 2018). Rashi adds that that Moshe ensured that Joshua understood what he was getting himself into. As a final point, Moshe has already set up the precedent of teaching the elders as he had done in Exodus 19:04,07. On all of this, Ramban stresses the survival of the Jews is based on the continuity of Moshe's leadership.

---

[35] The Great Assembly consisted of 120 scribes, sages, and prophets, which existed from the early Second Temple period (around 516 BCE) to the early Hellenistic period (333–332 BCE)

[36] Mensch is Yiddish word meaning a person of honor and integrity, like the familiar phrase, "(s)he's such a person"

A narrative as part of the legacy

Future generations who did not have direct experience with Moshe or the events of those days would need something tangible on which to grasp. In Numbers 32:03, it states that Moshe wrote down all the journeys of the past 40 years. In fact, Moshe assigned names to various places as a reminder. As one example, in Numbers 11:34 many people died because of Hashem's anger at the ungrateful complaining about the lack of meat. Thus, Moshe called the place Kibroth Hattaavah (graves of craving). In Deuteronomy 11:03, Moshe names a place "Taberah" (a burning) to remind the Israelites that this is where Hashem's fire burned against their misdeeds. Based on various sages, Rashi brings all this was to establish the narrative as part of the legacy. Ramban explicitly states that this was for the future generations who would not have the benefit of firsthand experience.

Ritual as part of the legacy

As a companion to the narrative, rituals were also established. Rabbi Sacks (Sacks, 2016, p. 154) makes note of the transformative event when Moshe brings down the second set of tablets (Exodus 34:01). The Israelites had done repentance and gained atonement for the sin of the golden calf. Rabbi Sacks brings this legacy event was perpetuated by turning it into a ritual which is now Yom Kippur[37]. Further, at the end of Moshe's life (in Deuteronomy 05:01) he instructs the Israelites, "Hear, O Israel, the statutes and ordinances which I speak in your ears this day, and *learn them*..." The Rav

---

[37] Alongside the related holiday of Rosh Hashanah, Yom Kippur is one of the two components of the "High Holy Days" of Judaism. It is also the last day of the Ten Days of Repentance

points out that nowhere did Moshe propose learning as an intellectual exercise (Soloveitchik, 2018); the learning here was to be able to teach others, to maintain the legacy.

Thus, we see that establishing a legacy is key to continuity of the principles of a leader. A key part of the process for doing so is making a clear leadership chain. Just as important, establishment of rituals to memorialize the initial principles serves future generations.

Humility and introspection

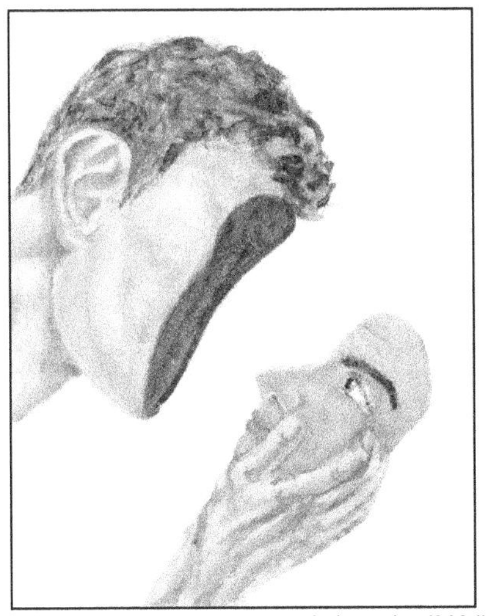

"Introspection" by Shayna Rochel Towler (2024)

Starting with the assumption of humility

Moshe's humility can be seen throughout his life. Early, when receiving the task to redeem the Israelites from Egyptian servitude, he was too humble to think he was an appropriate choice (Exodus 03-04). After the redemption, in Numbers 12:03, the Torah explicitly tells us of his humility stating, "Now this man Moshe was exceedingly humble, more so than any person on the face of the earth." Given we have selected Moshe as a paragon of leadership, any attribute worth being called out so overtly in the Torah should perhaps be investigated thoroughly. Interestingly, the verse declaring Moshe so humble directly follows a verse where Moshe's brother and sister were speaking ill of him and questioning his leadership. Dr. Cohen brings that the actual text is understood that Moshe certainly heard his siblings speaking but did nothing to defend himself against the slander (N. J. Cohen, 2008, p.126). In short Moshe's humility can be seen by the fact that however quick he is to defend the Israelites, he is hesitant to do the same for himself

Moshe was not only humble himself, he taught humility. In his final days, Moshe warns the Israelites about becoming too prideful or sanctimonious about their accomplishments (Deuteronomy 08:11 and Deuteronomy 09:01). Although not directly referring to Moshe, The Rebbe, addressing his own followers on the occasion of his 85th, birthday in 1985 commented that:

> *"Immodesty [lack of humility] is one of the greatest destructive attributes in human nature. It is the root of all inappropriate behavior."* (Jacobson, 2002, p. 170).

In another conversation when The Rebbe was asked whether it is more important to search for a judge who has extensive knowledge or humility. His cogent answer was:

> *"Surely, a judge must have the appropriate knowledge and experience. But it is more important to rely on someone [judge or **leader**] who will honestly consider all the arguments, someone who has the **humility** to eliminate his own state of thinking while dispassionately considering each side"* (Jacobson, 2002, p. 266)

The Rebbe was making the point that humility is one of the most fundamental characteristics of a leader, who will never seek honor for himself but rather for the principles he has chosen. We gain further practical insight into what it means to be humble, looking at how this trait manifested itself in our archetypical leader.

An assumption of misunderstanding

In Exodus 03:03, Moshe talks to Hashem by the burning bush. There Moshe uses an interesting phrase , "let me turn away" (אָסֻרָה־נָּא). Rashi brings that Moshe realized he was not comprehending the essence of Hashem and was trying to approach it from a different direction (maybe both physically and spiritually). This is supported by Hashem telling Moshe just two verses later in Exodus 03:05, "come no closer." Rambam brings that Moshe was not at the right level to understand, as he would be later when he received the Torah. Albeit he was talking to the Almighty, this represents a manifestation of humility in which Moshe was assuming that his lack of understanding was the issue, not the message itself.

Recognizing the greatness in others

Sincere humility inherently implies that one recognizes that others exist who are greater than oneself, a characteristic seen in Moshe. In Exodus 07:01-02, Hashem tells Moshe that he will tell Pharoah all that Hashem commands but then goes on to say that Aaron his brother will be "his speaker." Rashi points out that the Hebrew word used in the text for "your speaker" (נְבִיאֶךָ) also means "your prophet; " i.e., not only will Aaron literally speak for Moshe as we see in the narrative but he will provide a moral compass as a prophet does. We see displays of humility again when Moshe's father-in-law, Jethro, came to meet him in the desert and Moshe bowed down to him and kissed him (Exodus 18:07). Here was the man who was equal to the entire generation and the only one who had spoken "face-to-face" to Hashem himself (Numbers 12:08) but still lowered himself to those around him.

Taking advice from others

Another indication of Moshe's humility is his willingness not only to show respect for others but also to be willing to take guidance on proper conduct. Two examples come from Moshe's interaction with his father-in-law Jethro. In the first example, on hearing what Hashem has done for the Israelites, Jethro responds "Baruch Hashem[38]" (Exodus 18:10). This phrase has been part of the Jewish vernacular for the last 3500 years. This transpired only due to the fact that Moshe recognized this as praiseworthy. Interesting, Torah Temimah (Epstein, 1989) brings from Tractate Sanhedrin 94a that it was to Moshe's discredit that this proper conduct did not come from himself and that he had to learn it from one lower than himself, even though he mended his ways and adopted the practice. Later in the narrative, Jethro saw that Moshe was overwhelmed with the questions and legal struggles of the Israelites. Jethro again offered advice by suggesting that Moshe set up lower courts and even went so far as to tell Moses he should ask Hashem about this (Exodus 18:19). Moshe humbly accepts this advice and acts on it right away. A final example comes from the daughters of Zelophehad of the tribe of Menashe-Mahlah, Noa, Hoglah, Milcah, and Tirzah. The daughters approached Moshe because their father had died without a son to inherit land in Canaan, leaving them without; their argument was that they should inherit nonetheless The Rebbe brings that Moshe recognized that he could be biased because Zelophehad had been a loyal follower and thus recused himself from making this decision on his own. Moshe

---

[38] Colloquially, this is like the English phrase, "Thank G-d"

went to Hashem a couple of verses later, who "agreed" with the daughters' argument and thus it became a new law. Had it not been for Moshe's strong self-esteem and humility, we would not have this exemplary behavior of being willing to take unsolicited guidance from anyone and seek out advice when appropriate (it is noteworthy that Moshe did not consult with Hashem on all decisions that he had to make as a leader).

Desire for others' success

Beyond recognizing greatness in others, and willing to take good advice from anyone, a truly humble leader desires the success of others. We see this in Numbers 11:29 where Joshua comes to complain to Moshe that Eldad and Medad were prophesizing in the camp instead of joining the other elders with Moshe. Although Ramban agrees Eldad and Medad were acting above their station, Moshe corrects Joshua by asking him on whose account is he being a zealot and says he wishes all Israelites could reach such heights.

Consideration of even unwarranted criticism

As a final example of evidence of Moshe's humility, we look to his introspective nature upon receiving criticism. In Numbers 12:03, the Torah relates the story of Moshe's siblings (Miriam and Aaron) gossiping about him and questioning his leadership. Immediately after relating the story, the Torah says Moshe was exceedingly humble. This description explains why he prayed for his sister's recovery from the divine punishment for this act and seems to be evidence that he considered the criticism, even if untrue. Later, after the rebellion of Korach, Moshe is quite distressed and calls out to Hashem saying, "I did not take a donkey or wrong them" (Numbers 16:15).   Rashi points out that he had a right to request donkeys for his trouble of coming back to redeem them[39].   Ramban brings not only had he not taken donkeys, he also had not taxed them as many leaders would nor had he asked them to do any work for him. Thus, we see that Moshe considered even unwarranted criticism due to his humility.

[39] Torah Temimah (Epstein, 1989) makes the point that when the 72 sages were asked by King Ptolemy to transcribe the Torah (into Greek in Alexandria, Egypt in the 200's BCE), each one translated this as " not one desirable object of theirs have I taken", showing how fundamental this concept was to Moshe as a leader

Patience and perseverance

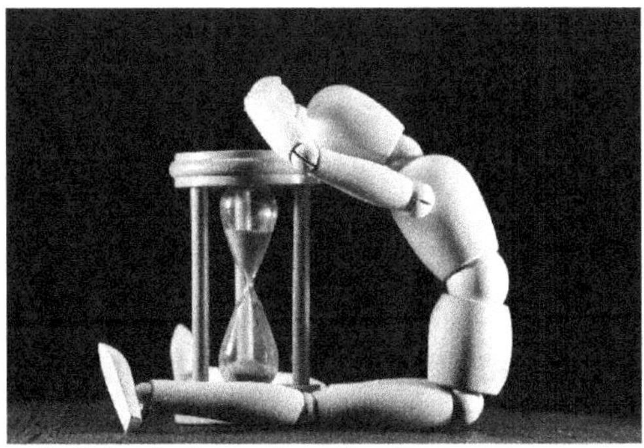

Copied under license from https://www.vecteezy.com

It may appear self-evident that patience and perseverance are prerequisite attributes of any potential leader. Rabbi Grumet points out that, throughout the narrative, there are many failures that would otherwise crush a normal individual but Moshe perseveres (Grumet, 2014, p.139). Dr. Cohen makes note that this is even in the face of what seems to be Moshe's own self-doubt (N. J. Cohen, 2008, p. 35). We can see the many ways this manifested itself through Moshe's tenure. During the redemption of the Israelites from the hand of Pharoah, Moshe waited for one plague after the other until Pharoah finally acquiesced to freeing the Israelites (Exodus 07-12). During the subsequent sojourns in the desert, Moshe endured multiple complaints and lack of faith in his leadership but continued, even when Hashem offered to be rid of the people he is trying to lead. Dr. Cohen makes note of one particular incident after the Israelites had just escaped the pursuing Egyptian army by the splitting of the sea and were already complaining about the lack of drinkable water, despite having just seen what could be done (Exodus 15: 22-27). Dr. Cohen points out that Moshe does not take this personally and just perseveres with his mission and solves their problem (N. J. Cohen, 2008, p. 64). The Rav suggests that the people had already forgotten [or not internalized] the full vision (Soloveitchik, 2008). It is also possible that they had internalized only the redemption aspect but not the full culture change. Rabbi Sacks (Sacks, 2016, p. 219) notes that Moshe's perseverance is not only in the face of personal setbacks but also in the face of unmet expectations of the people he is leading. As another example of Moshe's patience and perseverance, The Rav references Numbers 12:15 where Miriam had been placed outside the camp until she is healed from tzara'at[40]. Although Moshe could have easily, and perhaps understandably, encouraged the people to move on and have Miriam follow outside the camp, he patiently waited for her to heal (Soloveitchik, 2018). Perhaps one of the strongest examples is Moshe's determination even after he realizes he will not be the leader to see the mission to its end (Grumet, 2014, p. 168); as Rabbi Grumet brings (Grumet, 2014, p. 139) from Pirkei Avot[41] 2:21, "even if the task is not ours to complete…we are not relieved from doing that which is in our reach."

Conceivably more important than the attribute itself, is the effect it has on the leader. In Exodus 07:12, Hashem says of Moshe, "he is [supremely] loyal in my house." Rabbis Sacks (Sacks, 2016, p. 219) comments that despite Moshe's disappointment in the Israelites he

---

[40] Numbers 12:01-16: This story tells of how Miriam and Aaron sinned in speaking falsely against Moshe, and the punishment was for Miriam to a suffer skin disease referred to as tzara'at

[41] Pirkei Avot (literally "Chapters of the Fathers," also known as "Ethics of our Fathers") is a tractate of the Talmud and the only tractate with almost no laws, consisting instead of short statement of advice, ethics, and wisdom.

continued to persevere and argue on their behalf (for example in Exodus 05:22, Exodus 32:32, Numbers 14:19, Numbers 16:22, Numbers 12:13). In Moshe's final days the Torah states that Moshe was "120 years old and his eyes were undimmed." He had the same vigor as a younger man. Rabbis Sacks (Sacks, 2016, p. 68) brings in summary that leadership is marked by failure but the perseverance of a true leader builds him. At 120, Moshe had endured to become the supreme leader.

Maintaining proper perspective

Copied under license from https://www.vecteezy.com

Maintaining perspective is called out separately here to see how it manifests itself as understanding the proper timing. At the forefront of Moshe's leadership, he is talking to Hashem through the burning bush. As has been pointed out elsewhere, he says "let me turn away" (Exodus 03:03). Rashi explains that this is not turning away completely but a self-recognition of not having the proper perspective. Indeed, The Rav points out that Moshe had run away from Egypt thinking that the Israelites were unredeemable due to centuries of slavery and oppression (Soloveitchik, 2013, pp. 78-79). To correct this misperception, Hashem instructs Moshe to go down to Egypt and "see" all the wonders Hashem will put in his hand (Exodus 04:21). Rashi comments that he will "see" really means Moshe will need the perspective to "see" that all that has and will transpire is part of a bigger plan. Ramban adds that Moshe needs to be prepared for rejection. Moshe will need the perspective of knowing there is a bigger plan.   Much later in the narrative, when the Jews were trapped by Pharoah's pursuing army, they started praying, to which Hashem says to Moshe, "Why do you cry out to me" (Exodus 14:15).   Rashi points out that this was not a time for prayer and reflection (prayer being a reflexive verb in Hebrew) but a time for action, and that Moshe was being told to reevaluate his perspective of the situation. Ramban comments that Hashem is chastising Moshe saying, "you already know what to do," to look at this situation in a different way and stop thinking about it from his current perspective. As a final example, Moshe asks Hashem to see "his glory" immediately after the debacle of the golden calf and the sincere repentance of the Israelites (Exodus 32). Rashi brings that now was an opportune time since Moshe had just "convinced" Hashem to not kill off the Israelites. His perspective proved to be accurate as he was indeed shown the "back" of Hashem (Exodus 33:23). Thus, although Moshe had to be corrected throughout his life on perspective, we see how significant this attribute is, that it led to Moshe "seeing" Hashem.

Delivering hard messages and making difficult decisions

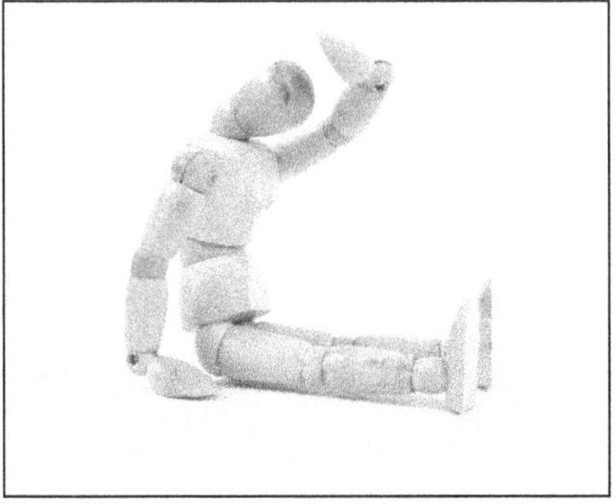

Copied under license from https://www.vecteezy.com

Part of being a strong leader is being able to deliver hard messages and making difficult decisions. Sometimes this is communicating the natural consequences of a behavior. Sometimes it is communicating that for some acts there are no second chances. In either case, the rationale is as important as the consequences themselves.

In Numbers 16:28, Moshe says that those involved in the rebellion of Korach[42] will be swallowed up by the earth. The Rebbe focuses on the fact that Korach's rebellion was not for "the sake of heaven;" he was a reactionary leader making decisions based on his own emotional feeling which expectedly led to a disastrous end. Rashi focuses on verse 29 in which Moshe states that it was necessary for these men to die an unnatural death proving not only that he himself was the true

---

[42] In Numbers 16:01–40 Korach rebelled against Moshe along with Dathan and Abiram and 250 co-conspirators. The 250 co-conspirators were punished for their rebellion when they offered incense to God in fire pans and the heavenly fire from the incense pans consumed all 250 of them. Korach from the tribe of Levi and his allies Dathan and Abiram from the tribe of Reuben were also punished when God caused the ground to split open beneath their feet, swallowing them, their families, anyone associated with Korah, and all their possessions.

leader and the punishments are from Hashem but more importantly that their manner of death is the natural consequence of their behavior. In the subsequent verses (Numbers 17:06) the people began to rebel against Moshe for having killed Korach and his followers. The Rav points out that this decision was not taken lightly and was a difficult message only after having warned the rebels (Soloveitchik, 2018). Despite having to deliver this tough message, Moshe says it is "not from my heart" to want this, showing that having empathy is not separate from understanding the need to deliver difficult messages. Dr. Cohen makes the points that this decision came about only due to Korach and his followers of their misguided ways (N. J. Cohen, 2008, p. 139) and he devotes an entire chapter to making difficult decisions. Toxic personalities must be reformed or removed.

A second example comes from when the Israelites were about to enter Cannan, the promised land, before which they sent 12 men to spy out the land for the pending conquest. After 40 days the spies came back and gave an unnecessarily bad report regarding the chances of a successful campaign (Numbers 13:01-33). In "frustration," Hashem told Moshe he would annihilate the Israelites and rebuild the nations from Moshe himself (Numbers 14:12). This would appear as the natural consequence of their behavior based on Hashem having warned them previously in Leviticus 26:21, "And if you treat Me as happenstance, and you do not wish to listen to Me, I will add seven punishments corresponding to your sins." Still, Moshe made a logical petition to Hashem of how this would appear if he destroyed those he just redeemed and thus the Israelites were allowed to live, although that generation of adults would not be allowed to enter the promised land. After the Israelites realized their grave error, they wanted to proceed to conquer the land (Number 14:41). Moshe warns them that in this case there are no second chances. They do not listen and are slaughtered in their attempt. Thus, we see that although Moshe had the compassion to soften the blow of their lack of faith in the conquest of Canaan, that only went so far; at some point there are no second chances.

Another particularly striking example of Moshe delivering a hard message occurs in Numbers 20:26-27. There, Moshe tells Aaron that he will die and not see the promised land because he was partially responsible for Moshe's own sin of hitting the rock instead of addressing it as instructed by Hashem[43]. Rashi points out how hard this was for Moshe to take Aaron to Mount Hor to divest him of his priestly garments. The point worth further consideration is that there were consequences for Moshe's actions, not only for himself but for Aaron as well.

Perhaps the most difficult messages Moshe had to deliver are told in the events in Numbers 25:05 and in Deuteronomy 13:18. In Numbers 25:05 Moshe is confronted with the unpleasant situation where many of the Israelites were lured into worshipping the idol Baal Peor. The text tells us that Moshe instructs the judges to let each kill his fellow Israelite who was "attached" to the idol. Torah Temima

---

[43] This event occurred at the so-called "Waters of Strife" (Mei Meribah) in Numbers Chapter 20. There the Israelites needed water. Hashem commanded Moshe to "*speak* to the rock before their [the Israeli's] eyes, and it will give its water." Instead, being frustrated with the Israelite's lack of faith, "Moses raises his hand and *strikes* the rock twice with his staff. Water gushes forth, and the people and their cattle drink."

brings that even in this situation, it was clear that Moshe was looking for a way out. The Hebrew word used for "attached" (הַנִּצְמָדִים) also means "air tight seal," meaning Moshe only wanted this for those who had committed the most serious of offenses and Moshe much desired their repentance over capital punishment. In fact, Ramban brings from Tractate Sanhedrin 18a that 78,000 were eligible for the death sentence but the judges were able to secure repentance from most resulting in only 2 being killed by each judge as suggested by The Rebbe. In Deuteronomy 13:18, Moshe is speaking to the command to completely destroy a city that is determined to be evil. The Rav brings that a leader must recognize those who are unredeemable and remove the seed so it does not grow (Soloveitchik, 2018). Today this is more likely to result in the firing of a toxic personality. Nonetheless, we see that Moshe is willing to deliver the hard message but only after having exhausted all other possibilities.

In the end of Moshe's leadership, as he is preparing the Israelites for his eminent death, he warns the Israelites in the harshest of terms saying, *"And it will be, if you do not obey the Lord, your God, to observe to fulfill all His commandments and statutes which I am commanding you this day, that all these curses will come upon you and overtake you"*, whereafter he lists the many maladies that will befall the people if they do not obey (Deuteronomy 28:15). Rabbi Abbe (Abbe, 2023, p. 156) on the beginning of the book of Deuteronomy posits the question why Moshe waited until the end of his life to bring these difficult but critical messages. He cites Rashi who makes the point that Moshe waited until right before his death to do this and

Sifsei Chachamin[44] who says the continuous rebuke would have generated bad feelings, even hatred and rebellion. Rabbi Abbe correlates Moshe's behavior with Carnegie principle of "relationships" (Carnegie, 2022)

---

[44] Sifsei Chachamim is a supercommentary on Rashi's commentary on Chumash. Written by Shabbetai ben Joseph Bass (1641–1718) in Amsterdam, it is mostly a collection of other commentaries, in addition to the author's own insights, meant to give a basic understanding of Rashi.

Self-sacrifice and courage

Copied under license from https://www.vecteezy.com

Moshe's courage and self-sacrifice are evident from the beginning of his journey. As pointed out by Dr. Cohen, the first example we see of Moshe being courageous is in Exodus 02:11-12 when he killed the Egyptian taskmaster who was beating an Israelite slave (N. J. Cohen, 2008, p. 4). The risk of this act was clear after the fact in that he was forced to flee Egypt fearing capital punishment, settling in Midian.

Moshe could have easily stayed in Midian with his wife and new family but instead returned to Egypt to confront Pharoah and convince the Israelites to leave, both of which had their risks. In Exodus 18:05, it says that Jethro came to visit Moshe in the wilderness with Moshe's wife and children. This is mentioned to point out the sacrifice he was making by leaving them in Midian during his travails in Egypt. Indeed, the Rav states that a leader like Moshe is a person who will by necessity retreat from society to some extent, into seclusion and loneliness (Soloveitchik, 2008, p. 80)

In Exodus 32:32, Hashem suggests destroying the Israelites because of his anger over the sin of the golden calf, and starting anew with Moshe and his family. To this proposal Moshe famously states that he did not want to be mentioned in the Torah if this were the case. The Rav points out that the fact that he was willing to essentially erase his whole existence demonstrates the capacity and degree to which Moshe was willing to sacrifice for others (Soloveitchik, 2013, p. 187).

In Numbers 31:01-03, Hashem tells Moshe to strike the Midianites for luring the Jews into idol worship after which he would be "brought in unto your people" (i.e. die). Rashi points out that Moshe could have easily prolonged his life by waiting to strike the Midianites but did what was clearly best for the people despite the huge impact to himself.

In Deuteronomy 01:37, Moshe tells the people that he will not be allowed to enter Canaan because of their actions when they provoked him at the "waters of strife" (Numbers 20:01–13) where Moshe, in his frustration with the Israelite's constant complaining, struck a rock for water instead of speaking to it as he was commanded. The Rav suggests that if his followers had loved him as much as he loved them, they would not have rebelled, and Moshe might not have had to sacrifice his leadership to the fulfillment of the mission.

In Deuteronomy 05:27, Moshe is recounting the story of the giving of the Ten Commandments where the Israelites complained after hearing only the first part that it was too much for them to bear and asked that Moshe listen for them. Moshe was told by Hashem to tell them to "return to their tents" and He would indeed communicate the rest to him directly. The Rav sees this "returning to their tents" as a metaphor for a leader at this level. The Israelites were free to go back to their everyday lives but Moshe was allowed no such privilege.

As the leader, Moshe no longer had children of his own as the entire nation of Israel were his children.   The Rav brings one proof from Numbers 11:12 when the people were complaining about the lack of meat and Moshe expresses that he did not expect to be a nursemaid to the Israelites, but he indeed had become a "mother" to the entire nation (Soloveitchik, 2013, p. 180).   The Rav brings further proof from when census was taken after 40 years of wandering, noting Moshe's children are not even mentioned (Soloveitchik, 2018).   As a final example, Rabbi Lapin (Lapin, 2014, p. 3) points out to the text in Deuteronomy 31:07 where Moshe charges Joshua with taking over and says, "be strong and have courage. "   This is not only significant because of the plain meaning of the words but also because Moshe is conveying that being a leader is not a popularity contest.   Doing what is right is not always popular and may cost one in either a tangible or intangible way.   Dr. Cohen states pointedly, an "individual who aspires to leadership must be willing to sacrifice (N. J. Cohen, 2008, p. 9). As stated by the late American hero, Senator John McCain (McCain & Salter, 2008), this is the very definition of courage, doing what is right despite the potential personal cost.   Indeed, in discussing the American tradition of world leadership, The Rebbe said:

> *"Certainly, those Americans who have been elected to public office will consider their privilege and duty to show what America and Americans stand for.   To be sure, such action is not always universally popular but do not all deeds of virtue and duty require courage?"*(Jacobson, 2002, p. 169).

Finally, Rabbi Abbe correlates this behavior with Covey's principle of "avoiding excuses" (Covey, 1989).

Testing followers

A leader is also a teacher, raising the next generation of leaders to create a "living legacy" as stated elsewhere. One key aspect of teaching is to test the students. An example of a successful test is brought by Rabbi Sacks (Sacks, 2016, pp. 115-119) who says that after the sin of the golden calf (Exodus 32:01-06), Moshe tested the Israelites to show they were redeemable by allowing them to contribute to the tabernacle. Afterwards he blessed them (Exodus 39:43). In a second example (Leviticus 10:16-17), Moses is inquiring of the sons of Aharon (Elazar and Ithamar) about a halachic (legal) issue in front of their father, Aharon. This created the test/opportunity for the sons to defer to their father as they appropriately did.

The most famous test is when Moshe sends the spies to scout out the land before the pending conquest (Numbers 13:03). It is clear he is testing the Israelites although the nature of the test is not as clear. Rashi comments that we recognize it is a test because of its being placed next to Miriam's sin[45]; the spies should have learned the evil of spreading false reports. In tractate Sotah 34b, it states that the fact that the Israelites even requested to send spies shows a lack of faith, especially since it was promised as a land flowing with milk and honey (Exodus 03:08). This suggests they failed even before the "test." However, Torah Temimah suggests that asking to spy out the land was not the sin since we are not to rely on miracles, which leaves the unnecessarily bad report as the actual sin. Finally, The Rebbe brings

---

[45] See previous footnote on tzara'at

that every mitzvah (commandment) has two parts, explicit and implicit; the explicit is about WHAT you do and the implicit is about HOW you do it, giving the partisan a chance to show adherence to morals and ethics. From The Rebbe's point of view, it seems the test was more about HOW they conveyed what they found (tone) rather that the facts themselves. Thus, although there are differing opinions on what was being tested, this was the most consequential test for the generation that was redeemed from Egypt.

TRAINING STRATEGY TO BECOME A LEADER

Is there a strategy?

As we come to the final section of this work, one may ask whether there *is* a strategy to becoming a leader, or if leaders are born as such. The nature vs. nurture aspect of leadership has long been debated. Rabbi Sacks (Sacks, 2016, p.139) suggests, based on a biblical approach to leadership, that "people do not become leaders because they are great, they become great because they are leaders. " That is, they are willing to go beyond what they are naturally capable of doing. This was the story of Moshe himself and his message to the Israelites. Rabbi Grumet describes Moshe's transformation as moving from a man tied to the Vision to a man of the people; i.e., he grew into his role (Grumet, 2014, p. 79). Indeed, in Deuteronomy 11:26-28 Moshe says to the Israelites, "See, I am setting before you a blessing and a curse…" Moshe is defining the strategy to succeed toward the Vision he has communicated, that following the tenets in the Torah and adopting the leadership attributes emphasized there.   The question for today is how to apply this message three millennia later.

Focus on key principles

As elucidated by Rabbi Grumet (Grumet, 2014, p. 15) much of becoming a leader is about change in oneself, a transformation. Taken one step further, this would indicate that, in aiming to be a leader, focusing on the attributes one desires is a key component of any cogent strategy.   Not everyone agrees with this premise, that one should focus on leadership qualities to become a better leader (Brown,

2008). But, on page 61 of his book Rabbi Grumet quotes Christopher Hodgkinson, "If an unexamined life is not worth living, the unexamined value [i.e. personal TPP[46]] is not worth having." The key to **beginning** to train oneself is to have the humility for self-assessment and determining the gaps between one's current profile and one's target profile.

Self-examination is just the beginning. As Rabbi Grumet points out (Grumet, 2014, p. 15), "[Moshe] did not start out as a great leader and in fact did not start out as a leader at all." His evolution took place over four decades, the details of which we only know a small percent. Nonetheless, from various sources in the Torah, we learn that leadership development comes from focusing on the key principles. For example, in Numbers 08:02 Moshe is instructing Aaron how to light the wicks of the candelabra in the Temple, that the wicks should face the "face" (center). The Rebbe brings from Gur Aryeh[47] that this was clearly not to bring light, else the wicks would be facing in all different directions. Rather, the point is to focus on the key principles (i.e., Hashem's will) even when performing "menial" tasks like the daily lighting of the Temple menorah. Later, in Numbers 12:08 Moshe tells the Israelites to "safeguard" the matters of the Torah. Rashi brings that this means studying the precepts to which you have committed yourself; i.e., study the attributes which are part of your personal TPP so that they become part of you. Lastly, Rabbi Abbe

---

[46] Target Product Profile, as defined earlier

[47] Judah Loew ben Bezalel, also known as the Maharal, wrote among other things, Gur Aryeh al HaTorah, a supercommentary on Rashi's Torah commentary. He is also the subject of a later legend that he created the Golem of Prague, an animate being fashioned from clay

(Abbe, 2023, p. 11) makes the point that behaviors are habit forming; i.e., if one strives to make the attributes of their TPP part of everyday behavior, it will become a habit. As the old saying goes, "the heart follows the deed." In summary, to realize the leader inside, one must internalize the attributes of one's personal TPP and make them a habit in everyday life.

Make a plan and stick to it

Study the principles. The Rebbe says, "A leader's followers…should be studying his teachings" (Jacobson, 2002, p. 117). Whether we choose Moshe or someone else as our archetypical leader, part of becoming that person is to study the TPP they have developed for us. As The Rav says, "…holiness does not arrive suddenly, it comes by…preparation." (Soloveitchik, 2018, commenting on Leviticus 08:33). The same can be said of leadership, it comes from preparation.

Use opportunities as they present themselves. When The Rebbe was discussing the chaotic nature of the second half of the 20th century, he had a common theme. That was, to transform the chaos and upheavals into a force for good (Jacobson, 2002, p. 199). In other words, use the challenges as learning opportunities to improve oneself and those surrounding for the leadership needed during difficult periods. Indeed, The Rav comments on Moshe's response to the burning bush ("let me turn now," Exodus 03:03), as his realizing that he had to get away from the pragmatic logic of a shepherd (as manager or his father-in-law Jethro's flock) and adopt a new philosophy altogether (Soloveitchik, 2018).

If the opportunities do not exist, one must create them. In Exodus 02:13, Exodus 16-17, Moshe left his palace home where he was raised in comfort and "went out" to the Israelite slaves to bear witness to their strife. As noted by Rabbit Grumet (Grumet, 2014, p.66), he had to leave what was comfortable for him and challenge himself. This was the start of his journey to becoming a leader. Dr. Cohen adds to this idea by noting that when Moshe rescued Jethro's daughters from competing herdsman and ultimately joined his clan, he was immersing himself in a completely unfamiliar setting, thus creating a growth opportunity (N. J. Cohen, 2008, p. 13). Moshe learned early on that being a leader is not only being a spiritual/inspirational figurehead but also getting involved in the everyday concerns of the people (Grumet, 2014, p.84)

Ensure a support network is in place. In Exodus 02:07, Moshe is found by Pharoah's daughter, Batsheva, floating in a basket the Nile where his mother had put him that he might survive Pharoah's decree that all Israelite boys be slaughtered. Moshe's sister, Miriam, observes this and offers to find a wet nurse since Batsheva wants to keep the baby, and calls him Moshe. The Rav points out that this is just the first of a lifetime of examples where Miriam is part of Moshe's support network (Soloveitchik, 2018); every leader needs their "Miriam(s)."

Without a doubt, there will be setbacks along the way. To avoid "burn-out" one should tackle this training in manageable portions. In Exodus 06:12, Moshe is seemingly having self-doubt about Pharoah listening to him since even the Israelites did not listen. The Rav suggests it was important at this point that Moshe only know about the redemptive part of the vision and not the culture transformation which would be even harder and could be overwhelming (Soloveitchik, 2008). In addition, Rabbi Grumet tells us that for Moshe to be the action-driven leader he became and deal with the many trials along the way, he had to be a person of tremendous inner strength and have the humility for introspection along the way (Grumet, 2014, p.128). When the Israelites were fleeing and were trapped by the Egyptian army (Exodus 14:10-16), Moshe tells them to "stand firm." Dr. Cohen suggests that he is telling the Israelites that ultimate success will come only if they subordinate their fears (N. J. Cohen, 2008, p.43). Indeed, Moshe raises his hands to split the sea demonstrating to the people that they must take action for something to happen (N. J. Cohen, 2008, p.47). Finally, in Leviticus 23:15 the narrative is speaking of the time between the holiday of Passover[48] and Shavous[49] as being "seven weeks, they shall be *complete*." The Rav offers that the use of the word "complete" is to emphasize the enormous task our archetypical leader has taken on, to completely transform slaves where time is not of consequence[50] to leaders where one must be ever-cognizant of how time is spent. Thus, the attribute of perseverance and spending time efficiently comes into play even as one trains to be that leader.

As mentioned earlier, when Hashem tells Moshe to go down to Egypt and "see" all the wonders he will perform (Exodus 04:21), the

---

[48] https://aish.com/passover
[49] https://aish.com/shavuot
[50] Because they can work more efficiently or less but their situation will not be affected either way

text is not simply speaking of physical sight. From Rashi, one must be cognizant of the bigger picture, the product, oneself as the future leader. As mentioned above, Ramban goes further to emphasize that there will be setbacks along the way. But, if one were to accidently miss a cup when pouring water, one would obviously not continue to spill the drink but would refocus and ensure the liquid hits the glass; it is no different here. Rabbi Abbe (Abbe, 2023, p. 46) in relation to Exodus 13:19[51] relates this approach to Covey's principle of "creating good habits" (Covey, 1989). In short, mimic Moshe's own journey; be strong, perseverant, and introspective.

Celebrate the win and move on

In Exodus 14:10-16, the Israelites just have crossed the sea and escaped their Egyptian pursuers. Once they reached the other shore, they began to sing. Dr. Cohen brings the traditional understanding that the people asked Moshe to sing but he pointed out to the Israelites that it was their opportunity to seize the chance to show their personal leadership, since it was they who ventured into the water even before the sea split (N. J. Cohen, 2008, p. 54). Dr. Cohen brings later from Exodus 12:22-27, that the tradition tells us after the celebratory song, the Israelites were happy to stay by the sea for a while rather than move on and venture back into the desert, but Moshe encouraged them to get up and go (N. J. Cohen, 2008, 60). Thus, while celebrating the wins along the way, one must be careful not to become complacent.

---

[51] Rabbi Abbe brings that the story of Moshe taking the bones out of Egypt while the Israelites were busying themselves with the spoils shows that he was focused on the overall plan/mission never losing site of the end game

FINAL THOUGHTS

If one were to wonder for whom this work is intended, it is for everyone because "Everyone must be a leader" and take responsibility for the demands of leadership (Jacobson, 2002, p. 170). In his first speech after taking the mantle as the next leader of the Lubavitch movement, The Rebbe declared, "I do not decline from helping but nothing…can replace personal responsibility;" i.e., for their own leadership (Jacobson, 2002, p. 177). Indeed, when Aaron lost his sons Nadav and Avihu due to their inappropriate behavior in the holy of holies, Moshe told him (and his remaining sons), "Do not leave your head unshorn and do not rend your garments (traditional signs of mourning)." Although this may be a confusing way for Moshe to "comfort" his grieving brother, The Rav explains that this was because the priests were a special community with much more expected of them (Soloveitchik, 2018). As pointed out by The Rav, a leader at the level of Moshe and Aaron are expected to never panic, never complain, never act out of black despair (Soloveitchik, 2013, p. 171). Everyone is accountable for his leadership in whatever capacity he may act.

An obvious question is how to increase the chances of success as a leader. Rabbi Grumet believes one of Moshe's key attributes was his adaptive leadership which has been mentioned above as one of Rabbi Sacks' key leadership attributes. As suggested by The Rav in his introduction to the book of Exodus (Soloveitchik, 2018), a leader is picking up wherever the people are standing, never starting from nothing, and must therefore adapt accordingly. We see that Moshe adapted his interaction with both Pharoah and the Israelites, making modifications to ensure the plan executes (Grumet, 2014, p. 177). In dealing with people specifically, Moshe realized that he had to change his approach to transform the people from slave culture to a people with a mission for which they are willing to fight (Grumet, 2014, p. 142). Even further, he had to adapt from "redeemer" to "king-teacher" as mentioned above.

Adaptation is not only based on internal circumstances. For example, Rabbi Grumet points out that in Numbers 20-21 there are a series of seemingly repeated setbacks such as being rebuffed by both the kingdoms of Edon and Sihon when the Israelites requested to simply pass through their kingdoms; in fact, the Israelites were attacked. The argument made is that Moshe *adapted* to the situation and used these external enemies to help unify the Israelites (Grumet, 2014, p. 146). And why was Moshe so successful adapting? Rabbi Grumet holds it was due to his empathy (Grumet, 2014, p. 187). Thus, we see the attributes are not stand-alone character traits but affect each other.

And what is the evidence of Moshe's adapting to the change in the Israelites? In Numbers 10:1 Moshe records the commandment to make two trumpets to summon the "congregation." The *two* trumpets may signify the two parts of the Vision, the redemptive first part (from slavery in Egypt) and the transformative second part (becoming people with a mission). In fact, The Rav suggests just this based on the use of the word "congregation" ("edah," הָעֵדָה) as opposed to "encampment" (machaneh, "מַחֲנֶה") which is used earlier in the narrative. The Rav brings that the Vision has both a redemptive part, fighting against something (in this case Pharoah), and a transformative part, the long-term Vision. While the fight can unify a group, it is destructive to continue to rely on this.   The leader must adapt be able to focus on the pending transformation.

And what is the timeline to becoming a leader? As stated earlier, the transformation seen in Moshe was not immediate. In fact, the narrative of Moshe's life and his evolution as a leader, covers a span of over four decades. In Rabbi Grumet's book, he presents the table below that illustrates the difference between earlier parts of the narrative to Moshe's version some four decades later. In fact, Rabbi Grumet posits that Moshe's life may teach us more about becoming a leader than being a leader (Grumet, 2014, p. 228), making the case again for training.

Moshe's version (Deuteronomy)	**Earlier version (Exodus, Numbers)**
God is eager to fulfill His promise to the Israelites, and encourages them to go up to the land He promised (1:6-8)	*God no longer wants* the people in His presence, and instead send an emissary to escort them to the land He promised (Exodus 33: 01-04)
Moshe is delighted that the people have grown numerically, and suggests he needs assistants (1:9-12)	*Moshe is overwhelmed* by the task of leading the people and cannot handle it alone (Numbers 11:10-15)
Moshe initiates and suggests the appointment of a judicial hierarchy (1:13-17)	*Jethro initiates* the establishment of a judicial hierarchy after seeing Moshe *struggling* under the weight of the people's need for guidance (Exodus 18:17-26)

copied with permission from (Grumet, 2014, p. 194)

One may ask how Moshe is viewed today, some thousands of years after his life. More than anything Moshe is seen ultimately as a teacher. This may seem surprising given the Torah itself refers to him as a king in Deuteronomy 33:05. The fact that he is commonly referred to in Jewish circles as "Moshe Rabbeinu" (Moshe our teacher) and not Moshe our redeemer or any other such name speaks to this concept (N. J. Cohen, 2008, p. 175; Soloveitchik, 2013, p. 198). In fact, The Rav refers to Moshe's primary final role at that of "king-teacher" (Soloveitchik, 2021, on Exodus 06:26). Thus, in the end, a good leader must evolve to be a good teacher as well.

Was Moshe's leadership successful? Did the Israelites transform under his leadership? The answer seems be yes, and no. In Exodus 21:13-17, the Israelites find themselves in need of water once again, but they take a very different approach than before. Instead of complaining to Moshe, they sang a song, "'Ascend, O well,' sing to it!" Dr. Cohen uses this a proof that the Israelites have grown as well under Moshe's leadership (N. J. Cohen, 2008, pp. 152-153). On the other hand, in Numbers 20:12, Moshe is told, "…you shall not bring this assembly to the land [of Canaan]…". The Rav points out that although Moshe was clearly successful in the redemptive part of the vision (i.e., redeeming them from slavery), he was not completely successful in the culture transformation, the Israelites did not internalize this part under Moshe. The Rav further points out that each leader must consider himself as a messenger but only for the part he is destined to play (Soloveitchik, 2018) . Thus, any leader's success is dependent not only on personal growth but also on those being led, but incomplete success is still success.

Given the challenge to become a good leader one may wonder why anyone would seek a high-profile position. Indeed, in Numbers 16, the Torahs relates the story of Korach who staged a rebellion, claiming that Moshe was power-hungry and had appointed himself over them. The Rav points out that it was the people who had appointed Moshe and Korach was merely seeking power and recognition (Soloveitchik,

2018). The lesson here is perhaps beware of those too eager to be the leader.

Given the challenges, it might not be surprising that many good people are hesitant to take on leadership roles. Indeed, if one is compelled to take on a high-profile leadership role, the sacrifice of such a choice must undoubtedly be considered. In Exodus 03:05, Moshe was told by Hashem at the burning bush, "take your shoes off because the place you are standing is holy." The Rav states that what was actually being said was that Moshe as the leader would need to cast off his private matters because his role as leader of the Israelites does not allow for personal concerns. Further, in Numbers 03:01, it states, "These are the descendants of Aaron and Moshe..." The Rav asks points out that Moshe's lineage is not delineated here in part because his leadership stopped with him. As the leader of all Israel, he belonged to everyone and was even somewhat estranged from his own family. Lastly, in Numbers 20:20 it says, "...Aaron had expired and the entire house of Israel wept for 30 days." The Rav notes how surprising it might seem that that Moshe was mourned only by a select group. He suggests the reason was that while Aaron was the loving, "fun uncle," Moshe was the disciplinarian (Soloveitchik, 2018). Being a leader means that one must feel a sense of existential crisis, that one's whole heart is committed to it (Soloveitchik, 2018, on Deuteronomy 11:13).

The introduction to this work approaches leadership from a "business approach," although such a topic is not limited solely to those in the business world. Indeed, part of the most famous prayer in

Judaism (the "Shema") is mentioned in Deuteronomy 06:06. In speaking of the Torah Vision it says it should be on your mind, "when you sit in your home, and when you walk on your way, and when you lie down, and when you get up." The Rav brings that leadership is all-encompassing, 24 hours a day, 7 days a week (Soloveitchik, 2018). There is no "business leadership," just leadership, thus the title, "for business and every day."

BIBLIOGRAPHY

Abbe, E. (2023). *Torah Leadership*. Mosaica Press, Inc.

Ben Nachman, M. (2010). *Ramban (Nachmanides): Commentary on the Torah*. Shilo Publishing House, Inc.

Brown, E. (2008). *Inspired Jewish Leadership: Practical Approaches to Building Strong Communities*. Jewish Lights Publishing.

Carnegie, D. (2022). *How to Win Friends & Influence People*. Simon and Schuster.

Cohen, A. R., & Bradford, D. L. (1990). *Influence without Authority*. John Wiley & Sons Inc.

Cohen, N. J. (2008). *Moses and the Journey to Leadership: Timeless Lessons of Effective Management from the Bible and Today's Leaders*. Jewish Lights Publishing.

Cope, K. (2012). *Seeing the Big Picture: Business Acumen to Build Your Credibility, Career, and Company*. Acumen Learning.

Covey, S. R. (1989). *The 7 Habits of Highly Effective People: Powerful Lessons in Personal Change*. Free Press.

Epstein, B. H. (1989). *The Essential Torah Temimah* (S. Silverstein, Ed.). Feldheim Publishers, Ltd.

George, B. (2003). *Authentic Leadership: Rediscovering the Secrets to Creating Lasting Value*. Jossey-Bass.

Goleman, D. (2006). *Working with Emotional Intelligence*. Bantam Dell (A Division of Random House, Inc.).

Grumet, Z. (2014). *Moses and the path to leadership*. Urim.

Herczeg, Y. (1999). *Sapirstein Edition Rashi: The Torah with Rashi's Commentary Translated, Annotated and Elucidated*. Artscroll / Mesorah Publications, Ltd.

Jacobson, S. (2002). *Toward a Meaningful Life: The Wisdom of the Rebbe Menachem Mendel Schneerson*. Harper Collins.

Lapin, D. (2014). *Business Secrets from the Bible: Spiritual Success Strategies for Financial Abundance*. John Wiley and Sons, Inc.

Maxwell, J. C. (2007). The 21 irrefutable laws of leadership: follow them and people will follow you. In *Thomas Nelson, Inc.* (Issue c). Thomas Nelson.

Maxwell John C. (2019). *21 Qualities of Leaders in the Bible: Key Leadership Traits of the Men and Women in Scripture*. Harper Collins Christian Publishing, Inc. .

McCain, J., & Salter, M. (2008). *Faith of My Fathers*. Harper.

Miller, C. (2003). *The Gutnick Edition Chumash: Five Books of Moses*. Kol Menachem.

Sacks, J. (2016). *Lessons in Leadership: A Weekly Reading of the Jewish Bible*. Maggid Books.

Scalia, A., & Scalia, C. (2017). *Scalia speaks: Reflections on law, faith, and lives well-lived*. Crown Publishing.

Seinfeld, A. (2010). *The Art of Amazement*. Jewish Spiritual Literacy.

Soloveitchik, J. B. (2000). *Family Redeemed: Essays on Family Relationships* (D. Shatz & J. Wolowelsky, Eds.). Toras HoRav Foundation.

Soloveitchik, J. B. (2008). *Abraham's Journey: Reflections on the Life of the Founding Patriarch* (D. Shatz, J. B. Wolowelsky, & R. Ziegler, Eds.). KTAV Publishing, Inc.

Soloveitchik, J. B. (2013). *Vision and Leadership: Reflections on Joseph and Moses* (D. Shatz, J. B. Wolowelsky, & R. Ziegler, Eds.). KTAV Publishing House, Inc.

Soloveitchik, J. B. (2018). *Chumash Mesoras Harav - Complete Chumash with Commentary Based on the Teachings of Rabbi Joseph B. Soloveitchik* (A. Lustiger, Ed.). OU Press.

Towler, E. (2022, September 25). *Becoming a Project Leader is Just Like Drug Development...Except When It Isn't*. Online Post to LinkedIn. https://www.linkedin.com/pulse/becoming-project-leader-just-like-drug-when-isnt-eric-towler%3FtrackingId=yh%252FAjR3%252BQ529bcMVjHxT8Q%253D%253D/?trackingId=yh%2FAjR3%2BQ529bcMVjHxT8Q%3D%3D

Willet, A. (2016). *Leading the Unleadable: How to Manage Mavericks, Cynics, Divas, and Other Difficult People*. Harper Collins.

INDEX OF BIBLICAL CITATIONS

About the author

Dr. Towler is a PhD-trained scientist and a PMP-certified drug development leader with over 30 years of experience in all facets of drug development. He has been directly involved in the launching of numerous novel therapeutics in various diseases such as Diabetes, Hemophilia and Oncology.

Dr. Towler is passionate about project management and attributes his own success not only to strong technical skill but also to leadership. Beyond his successful publication and patent record in scientific journals, he has also written articles focused on the leadership aspect. In addition, Dr. Towler is requested to present keynote addresses on yearly basis to project management conferences where usually focusing on the role of leadership in success.   In this work, Dr. Towler have taken his experience in project management and applied it to leadership itself.